Introduction to PC Computing: MS-DOS, GEM & BASIC on the PC200 & PC Compatibles

Patrick J. Hall

SIGMA PRESS
Wilmslow, United Kingdom

First published in 1989 by
Sigma Press 1 South Oak Lane, Wilmslow, SK9 6AR, England.

British Library Cataloguing in Publication Data
A CIP catalogue record for this book is available from the British Library.

ISBN: 1-85058-150-9

Typesetting and design by
Sigma Hi-Tech Services Ltd

Cover design by
Professional Graphics, Warrington, UK

Distributed by
John Wiley & Sons Ltd., Baffins Lane, Chichester, West Sussex, England.

PREFACE

How to read this book

There is no reason why anybody should not read this book from cover to cover in sequential fashion. It is possible, though, to read certain sections independently of the others. Each of these parts of the book has been written as a self-contained account of one specific area of interest and application. Whilst avoiding any needless repetition, each section does not require the reader to have worked through any of the other parts first. In this way the book should be useful as a source of reference relating to the different areas covered.

Although the formality of 'Part 1' etc. has been excluded, it may help to think of the material as belonging to six parts. Part 1 would then be chapters 1-2. Part 2 is formed by chapters 3-5. Part 3 consists of chapters 6-8 and part 4 of chapters 9-13. Parts 5 and 6 are then the final chapters 14 and 15 respectively.

Chapters 1 and 2 serve as a general introduction to the Sinclair PC, putting it into an overall context of contemporary personal computing. After this, chapters 3-5 deal with the GEM environment, which many users may prefer to MS-DOS. The important, and remarkably versatile Organiser, is discussed in chapters 6-8. The longest section then follows, with the account given of the Sinclair PC's MS-DOS operating system. This occupies chapters 9-13. A brief description of the programming language bundled with the computer, GW-BASIC, follows in chapter 14. This is intended to place the dialect into perspective and compare it with other BASICs. It is not meant to be even a sketchy introduction to BASIC, and is not a teach yourself guide. Nevertheless it should help the complete beginner to acquire a sufficient taste for the language and want to pursue it further. Finally, chapter 15 considers some of the application software the Sinclair PC owner might want to acquire and gives an account of integrated packages.

A personal note and acknowledgement...

Nobody can work without encouragement. The long hours at a keyboard, which computing usually entails, could prove disturbing if it were not for frequent pep talks from friends. These help enormously, even if by necessity via the phone while the

Amstrad 1512 is dumping hard copy to the Epson RX-80. For the time spent incarcerated and silent in the study, I apologise to my mother.

John Scriven, now of Portsmouth Polytechnic, must be thanked for all his early advice. Similarly Dr. Graham Beech of Sigma Press has been instrumental in the development of several books and generally encouraged me in both computing and authorship. He has regularly maintained almost as flexible an attitude towards deadlines, and the calendar, as I have. For this I am extremely grateful. Anna Head, also of Sigma Press, has assisted by editing the text. On a pragmatic note, the staff of Arkrain Ltd., a local firm, have been consistently informative when confronted by various appeals for help. Additionally, the customer service provided by Comet, the supplier of my Sinclair PC, has been excellent.

I must express gratitude towards Brother Cyril and Michael Bownass of St. John's College, Southsea for their implicit support during the development of this book. I have benefited as well from the comments offered by several of my students there, especially Jason Bowers, David Counsell, Sarah Hartridge, Michael Hills and Chris Melikian.

Finally, I shall always remember with affection the enthusiasm of the original, St Francis computer club, in particular Mark Beard, Pauline and Andrew Davis, Andrew Denahy, Lucy Hopgood, to whom this book is again fondly dedicated, and Michelle Willcocks. The spontaneity of their interest in computing provided an important personal incentive at the time and many happy memories since.

Contents

An Introduction to the Sinclair PC

Computer shows are incredible events. Despite their recent invention, they have become institutional. Perhaps excessively dominated by the young and the male, nevertheless they have a magical atmosphere redolent of Santa's grotto when you are a child, or the first freshers' tea party at university. They are especially exciting for those making a rare visit from the provinces. London is always so ugly from a carriage window. It yields its penance, however, as mounting excitement when familiar outlines rise against the horizon, till at last the terminus arrives and the rush begins for the tube.

The computer-obsessed visitor now meets peers amongst the commuters. Anoraks, clenched carrier bags and inevitable computer magazines signal the way through London Underground to the Show's location. Then the brutal architecture of the Barbican - how easy to feel a royalist! - or the tent-like extension at Alexandra Palace even add to the atmosphere of crowded excitement. More free carrier bags, free balloons and French tourists politely enquiring about 'flippy disks', all confirm that you have arrived.

The Earls Court show at which the Sinclair PC made an early appearance even sported a gentleman in a smart business suit outside. He was sitting at the top of a step ladder to reveal how a rival brand of computer could be used anywhere. Naturally the average British passer-by assumed it was a demonstration of a new sort of waterproof keyboard, or possibly suit...

The launch of a new machine

It was in such an atmosphere that the Sinclair PC was launched in the autumn of 1988. Everybody had arrived anxious to see the new range of Amstrad 2000 series of computers and it was a with a distinct feeling of disbelief that a new Sinclair machine was discovered as well. Admittedly it came from more distant regions of the globe than the original ZX micros, but it still had the traditional Sinclair appearance in sleek, Henry Ford black. Most important of all it possessed the streamlined logo, now embossed in scarlet, which had advertised more than a decade of electronic innovation.

IBM PC - compatible computers

The significance of the launch of this new Sinclair computer was, of course, that it was a genuine 'PC' rather than just a microcomputer. It contributed an important new entry into the existing field of IBM PC compatible machines. A world of wide ranging software was already available, just waiting for a such personal computer, cheap enough to occupy a niche in the home as well as the office.

Despite its relatively late move into the world of microcomputers, IBM had soon established the industry standard. Other manufacturers learnt to produce computers themselves that would take advantage of the commercial software being made increasingly available. If you wish to take computing seriously, owning an IBM PC-compatible machine is a vital step. The Sinclair PC is an obvious choice in this range of computers.

The many worlds of the Sinclair PC

The Sinclair PC can be used to play games, but obviously the sensible owner will wish to achieve much more than this. The computer is provided with both GEM and MS-DOS and is able to handle a vast variety of commercial and business software. The Organiser software presents a wealth of software in itself, including a very easy, though adequate database and a word processor suitable for many needs. The Sinclair PC can be used to develop programs in GW-BASIC. All these aspects of the computer are considered in the chapters that follow.

A Sinclair PC workstation

The author's first Sinclair computer was the fabled ZX81 which, though advertised as capable of controlling a nuclear power station, was compact enough to perch easily on the corner of an ordinary writing desk. A portable television was necessary, but even so the overall computing complex was extremely discreet and undemanding. The extra 16 K RAM pack and thermal printer, when eventually added, also placed only slight further pressure upon space.

The Sinclair machines which have appeared since have been almost as small. The Spectrum computer has only slowly increased in size as it has evolved into an increasingly sophisticated machine. Similarly the slim appearance of the Sinclair QL might have been part of the reason why it failed to succeed in its early foray into the world of serious business computing.

As a result of this ancestral diminutiveness, Sinclair owners may well have expected their Sinclair PC to be a characteristically compact micro. Once home and eased out of the polystyrene swaddling in the two boxes, however, it is obvious that it is a large machine. Theoretically it will take up more room than other popular IBM PC-compatible computers, like the Amstrad 1512, 1640 and even PC2000 series of computers.

The user manual supplied with the Sinclair PC instructs you to find a table four feet wide and three deep in order to set up the machine. Many people will be able to do this, of course, but many others will not. The more compact, modern home often does not have this sort of space available. You might have to locate your Sinclair PC in a small spare bedroom, or even in the corner of a living room. An additional large table, which will not be able to be used for anything else, is going to be a problem.

To save room it will be tempting to try and stack the monitor on top of the computer itself. The Sinclair PC seems just about strong enough to allow this sort of mishandling. It would, though, be an unwise thing to do. A better solution is probably to spend a couple of days building your own Sinclair workstation. The design should include a sturdy monitor plinth to bridge the main body of the computer. This will then have the advantage of being considerably smaller than the large table suggested and more capable of slotting into a free corner. Unless an especially cheap table is available, the small quantity of wood required will lead to a saving in cost. You will also have the psychological benefit of knowing that you really do intend to take computing that seriously...

Defeating the dust problem

Electrostatic dust precipitation, as recommended by industry, is unavoidably simulated by home microcomputers. It makes no difference how much you pride yourself on cleanliness, a micro simply appeals to every mote in the atmosphere to make a crash landing on its screen. An Amstrad 1512 after several hours word processing once even managed to capture a mosquito which flew too close! There is not a great deal that you can do about this while you are actually using the machine. You must make some effort, however, to avoid leaving your Sinclair PC unprotected the rest of the time. Dust is an enemy of disk drives, quite apart from being unsightly.

If you can think of no other solution, at least leave a light cloth over the computer, like the cosy proverbially flung on top of the parrot's cage. A more professional result is to purchase an official dust cover. These can look rather ugly, though, and almost give the impression that you are about to move house.

A very original approach to the problem is to construct a dust cover yourself. This is much less expensive than the type you buy and, with care, could look better as well. The only materials required are a few A3 size sheets of acrylic plastic, the type used for overhead projector transparencies, and some strong adhesive tape.

Care of your disks

It is important that your disks are well protected. Place your original software in a safe place after making the copies you are going to use. It is quite a wise idea to work with copies of the copies themselves. Never do anything with the initial four disks except making the back-ups.

Although three and a half inch disks look extremely secure, still store them carefully in a plastic box. Most computer dealers have these and, if you buy enough disks at once, you can also get them free. Remember to identify everything thoroughly with pull-off adhesive labels. Unidentified disks, with potentially valuable contents, can become one of the most annoying aspects of computing.

A brief overview of personal computing

Sometimes it is difficult to walk down the local high street without wondering if time travel does occur. Shop windows are crammed with various makes of personal computer, all tiny, with ludicrously low prices and sharing display space with mundane toasters and cameras. It is like a John Wyndham short story in which the hero is whisked into his own future self, fifty years hence, and is terribly disturbed by the existence and proliferation of plastic.

Immense computing power is available to anybody who is prepared to pay roughly the price of a television set. Home computers have been in existence long enough for children to find it hard to imagine how anybody could regard them as anything out of the ordinary. Yet an older generation was reared in awe of the electronic brains described, sketchily but impressively, in school encyclopaedias. For them computers were veiled in hierophantic mystery and so they now find it unbelievable that such machines can sit comfortably on a bedside table.

The advent of personal computing

How did such compression of size and price become possible? It was certainly not predicted by the nineteen fifties seers who confidently described the jet propelled cars and nuclear airlines to be inherited by the next generation. They failed to foresee the domestic computer. Even genuine scientist turned to science fiction, Isaac Asimov, assumed that the computers of the future would be near city-sized. It was quite possible to walk around inside his famed 'Multivac'. He misjudged the future, too, in giving his supercomputer a touchingly human personality. This feat is still well beyond the attempts of all computer scientists engaged in Artificial Intelligence research. Multivac's human traits are even more improbable, now, than appeared in the confident early days of the first mainframe computers.

Swords into ploughshares?

Sadly it has to be admitted that much of the research that led to our conveniently small and affordable computers resulted from the need to control military weapons with sufficient accuracy. There was no way in which the intercontinental missiles being developed could be made large enough to accommodate the huge computers then in existence. A way had to be found to reconcile the control systems required for a sophisticated, automatic rocket with the small volumes available inside its slender hull.

An initial scheme devised by the American manufacturer, Texas Instruments, was to build 'micromodules'. Note that this term has met the same demise as 'wireless set' and 'spaceman'. Modern technology is ruthless in its paring of dated jargon. A micromodule was a ceramic wafer upon which the various components needed for part of a computer's circuitry could be printed. A number of micromodules could then be wired together into a unit.

The microchip is born

Fortunately for the future history of computing, one of the firm's employees, Jack Kilby, devised a far more sophisticated method for achieving similar results. It occurred to him that not only the transistors needed for computer circuits could be made from semiconducting material, but also the other discrete electronic components required to connect them: the resistors and capacitors. His further conceptual leap was to realise that this meant whole sections of computer could be fabricated as one tiny unit on the very same slice of semiconductor. Once his idea had jelled, he turned from theory to practice and produced the world's first integrated circuit, to astound his amazed colleagues. At first his device must have seemed rather Heath-Robinson, held together with solder and wax. However in its centimetre long germanium wafer it contained five separate components needed for part of a working computer. The race towards today's miniaturisation had begun. Soon more elegant devices were being produced by other researchers, perhaps unfairly pushing Kilby's work into relative obscurity.

The impact of the space programme

In the late nineteen eighties, the media still love to talk about the space race between America and Russia, ignoring the fact that the two countries have adopted such different priorities in space research that comparison is somewhat futile. The only true competition occurred in the nineteen sixties. This was between President Kennedy's firm assertion, that Americans would walk on the Moon before the end of the decade, and the state of the computer technology necessary to achieve that goal.

This race between vision and realisation was closely run throughout. Thus the prototype computer built for the Gemini spacecraft, which preceded Apollo, weighed a full ninety eight percent of the design limit set by NASA engineers. Its shape was determined by the interior curvature of Gemini, its discrete electronic components sandwiched in place by epoxy resin, and it employed a rather primitive form of memory. According to astronaut Walter Schirra, it looked like a box of bent coat hangers. Nevertheless, the machine worked and it allowed the Americans to perfect the orbital rendezvous techniques required for eventual lunar landing.

By the time Armstrong and Aldrin landed at Tranquillity, their on-board computer could perform all the status checks and calculations required for insertion back into lunar orbit, but already the machine they used was quite primitive compared with the computational power now becoming available.

Domestic computers arrive

Personal computers could have been developed almost a decade before their commercial exploitation began. The fact that they did not appear that soon probably reflects a lack of public imagination. This seemed to need a cosy incubation period of increasingly powerful calculators before realising the imminence of a far mightier device.

America, of course, was first with the new product. The Altair 8800 personal computer was launched in 1975. Ironically it only created the new market, rather than dominating it, and soon faded before the fabled Apple. Characteristically, Britain took longer. Commodore PET computers began filtering across the Atlantic and into small firms about a year later, but it was not until 1980 that microcomputers really created much of a public impact. This was with the launch of the Sinclair ZX80, the first home computer to break the £100 barrier. A wise psychological move, this price brought the machine to the attention of people who would never have remotely considered a computer for the home. The ZX80 even featured as a major item on Independent Television News.

The rest, of course, is history. Many British microcomputers have flourished, and then disappeared rapidly, during the decade, some leaving a loyal ownership years after the machine itself ceased production. The Sinclair QL is an excellent example of this. It is, of course, rather reassuring that two of the earliest names, Acorn and Sinclair, have continued to have a significant presence in the domestic computer market.

The hardware and software

Personal computing has introduced an imaginative selection of new words into everyday speech. Wander into the right section of a department store and you will hear language seemingly purloined from old science fiction movies, as small boys knowledgeably discuss the latest micro with middle-aged female assistants. We have created a technologically aware milieu.

So many people now automatically interpret 'hardware' and 'software' in the computing sense that it is probably just as well that the traditional ironmongers shop never quite made it to the modern shopping mall. If it had, constant explanation of the merchandise would have been needed.

Everybody knows that the hardware is the machine itself, always hailed as the next best thing to a Cray supercomputer and inevitably costing 1p less than a multiple of £100. Software is simply the collection of programs you need to buy in order to do anything with the machine. Fewer people are certain exactly what 'operating system' means. However, if you are to get the best service from any computer, it does help if you know which operating system the machine has. Then you can begin to study exactly what it does.

The human 'operating system'

The way in which the average owner of a personal computer implicitly takes for granted the existence of the machine's operating system is fairly similar to our ready acceptance of the functioning of our body. We assume the autonomous working of our heart, lungs, nervous system and other bodily components without a moment's thought. It is only when we become excited, run to the top floor of a supermarket car park or listen to a sobering tv health programme, that we remember our heart. Yet that is a reasonably familiar part of the human machine. Imagine how odd it would be if one of the less obvious components went wrong. Then we would appreciate its normal behaviour. So should the computer user attempt to appreciate the secretive compliance of the machine's operating system.

Surviving without an operating system

Just such a physical catastrophe was described in sympathetic, yet inevitably grotesque, detail by the neurologist Oliver Sacks in his intriguing collection of true-life case studies, 'The Man Who Mistook His Wife For A Hat'. The initial chapter, which gave the book its title, subsequently became the libretto for a contemporary British opera, but it is the third chapter which reflects the importance of part of the human 'operating system'. Ironically it concerned a real life computer programmer, Christina. A healthy twenty-seven-year-old, and mother of two children, she succumbed to a rare condition in which part of her nervous system was rapidly destroyed. Her brain was still able to control her body. She was not paralysed. However the sensory feedback though which the various parts of the body automatically and continuously inform the brain of their position in space was lost. Normally we are all aware of exactly how each part of ourselves is arranged. You do not need to look in a mirror to know that you are standing up rather than sitting down. Children like to play a game in which they bring their finger tips into contact while keeping their eyes shut. This sort of ability we take for granted. It does, though, suppose a constant flow of information into the brain from the different parts of the body. The technical term is 'proprioception'. It was this that Christina had lost.

Polyneuritis which set in after a minor operation led to the destruction of the proprioceptive fibres needed for her sensory feedback. She could not stand unless she looked at her feet. If she wanted to hold something in her hands she had to look at them constantly. Muscle tone was wholly lost. Limbs overshot their expected positions. She said she felt weird and disembodied.

With time and patience, Christina leant to adjust to this strange disability of her nervous system. Gradually she managed to control her alien body in a conscious manner, relying upon the alternative feedback provided by her eyes. Never again able to feel, nevertheless she now leads a outwardly normal life. Yet the whole time she has to think out in explicit detail the instructions needed to give apparent spontaneity to her ghostly limbs.

Computers and job control languages

This brief excursion into physiology may make your Sinclair PC seem just a little more magical. You will appreciate its operating system. Before the development of operating systems for computers, programmers were obliged to think out every possible action for their machines in advance. Like Christina, they could take nothing for granted. Using unfriendly and austere Job Control Languages, they needed to instruct the hardware of their computers in every little step that was necessary to get the system up and running and able to execute the actual computer program that they wanted to execute. Such job control languages needed to specify the various tasks the basic hardware had to perform simply in order to be able to be able to function at the most primitive level. A limited number of commands would be used to tell the computer what should be loaded from memory, what working 'files' were needed, which devices should be connected etc., leading to a fairly opaque set of instructions rather like this small illustration:

```
LOAD  LANG
CREATE LANGSCRT * SET UP A SCRATCH FILE
ASSIGN 1,LANGSCRT * CONNECT SCRATCH FILE
```

The owner of the Sinclair PC200 should be thankful that it is no longer necessary to control a computer in such a fundamental way. The operating system is your salvation.

Controlling the system's resources

In order to understand the role of a computer's operating system, it is necessary first to regard a computer as a set of resources. These are not simply the actual hardware of the computer, the chips, disk drives, keyboard, monitor screen, printer and other devices, but also the program itself and data needed by the program. The operating system acts as the manager of all these resources. It decides when a particular one is required, perhaps directing output from monitor to printer, or accessing some further program located on a disk. It is a little like the ringmaster in a very busy circus. While using your Sinclair PC200, you will be especially aware of the autonomy of the operating system when the green lights come on, indicating that the disk drive is being accessed.

A supervisory program...

At the same time you must appreciate that the operating system is itself a program. It was written by a group of people who understood in great detail the way in which the computer functions. Unexpectedly, the manufacturer of a particular computer will not necessarily write the operating system for it. Certain types of operating system, like

MS-DOS, CP/M and UNIX, have become the standard adopted by manufacturers. The only extra detail that needs to be attended to is the adjustment of one of these operating systems to the given computer. This is necessary because the hardware for each type of computer will have been assembled in a different way.

Occasionally a new computer will emerge which does have a unique operating system, like 'QDOS' which appeared with the Sinclair QL, but this is not always an advantage. Just as it would now be difficult to persuade the British to drive on the wrong side of the road, so the operating systems which have become the basis of so many personal computers now exert a considerable influence on whatever else is introduced into the market. For example the very original Archimedes computer produced by Acorn nevertheless has a PC emulator to allow it to use the software originally written for IBM PC-compatibles.

The Sinclair PC's operating system

As you are aware, the Sinclair PC is one of the latest additions to the wide range of IBM PC-compatible machines. This means that like so many other microcomputers before, it has adopted the operating system chosen by IBM when that very large company entered the world of personal computing. As a result of being an IBM clone, your Sinclair PC automatically has a broad range of software available for its use. This makes far more sense than having a distinctive operating system of its own, which would not initially have a great deal of software available.

This IBM based operating system is called MS-DOS. It is certainly an investment to learn about it in detail because this will not only allow you to exploit your Sinclair PC to its full potential but also provide familiarity with the wide range of personal computers which use MS-DOS as their operating system. As already stated, a later section of this book investigates MS-DOS.

3

Looking at GEM

The operating system which controls the operation of your Sinclair PC is Microsoft's MS-DOS. This will be described in chapters 9-13 of this book. At first, MS-DOS can seem slightly less than user friendly and for this reason the Sinclair PC is also equipped with another piece of software called GEM (Graphical Environment Manager). This allows the various MS-DOS commands to be operated via a series of pictures on the screen, known as 'icons', together with the mouse which moves an arrow, or cursor, about on the screen. The non-typist is therefore able to enter information without undue strain. The cynical may, at the same time, suspect that GEM was the way its inventors, Digital Research, were able to reassert their influence upon the computer market. Until the IBM PC was packaged with Microsoft's MS-DOS, the leading operating system for small computers had been Digital Research's own CP/M, an acronym for 'Control Program for Microcomputers'.

Undoubtedly GEM does make life much easier for the Sinclair PC user, but you will still need to spend a little time learning just how to use it. Try to avoid the spite of those MS-DOS enthusiasts who unkindly regard GEM as an unfortunate blemish in the history of personal computing and an unnecessary return to pictorial representation.

The first step - mouse taming

Probably until now your only experience of mice, unless you live in an elderly block of flats, will have been Jerry in cartoons. Alas, no computer mouse is that intelligent. Accidentally knock your mouse with a clipboard and you will see its corresponding pointer on the screen scamper happily in quite the wrong direction.

In fact you will need to have a suitable surface to run your mouse to and fro and in small circular motions. The location of the mouse's socket under the keyboard suggests that the available flat surface should be on the right hand side of your Sinclair PC, but the lead is long enough for you to operate it on the left if necessary. The area should possess the correct tactile qualities to provide friction and interact with the ball without skidding. You may need to place a magazine under it if it is sliding rather than rolling. The affluent might even buy a special mouse mat, the latest toy appearing in computer dealers.

Do not panic if the ball falls out completely. This appears to be the only connection with traditional Sinclair 'RAM-pack-wobble' and, unlike that, is not fatal to whatever you are doing at the time. Be brave, reinsert the ball after a brief glimpse of the mouse's entrails, and tighten the ring fixing it in place with a sharp twist towards the word 'close' embossed in the plastic.

Beginning with GEM

When you use your back-up GEM disk for the first time you have to go through a special routine which will not need to be repeated, unless at some point you have to make another back-up copy from your original GEM disk.

You will have switched on your Sinclair PC and booted it with your copy of the MS-DOS disk. You then remove the MS-DOS disk but must put it nearby. It will soon be required again. Place your back-up copy of the GEM disk into the drive and type CD\ followed by the <ENTER> key, and then **GEM** <ENTER>. Then screen display will be like this:

```
A>CD\
A>GEM
```

You will see the following message appear on your monitor screen, boxed in completely by lines of asterisks. The way in which your single disk drive is referred to by two different letters will be referred to again in chapter 9. Remember also that in any reference to actual screen prompts, as here, the American spelling of the people who wrote GEM and MS-DOS will be retained:

```
****************************************************************
Updating GEM startup disk...
As your PC has only one floppy disk drive, you will see messages
on the screen instructing you when to insert either your
GEM Startup Disk or your MSDOS System Disk in the disk drive.

When you see the message:
 ''Insert diskette for drive B: and strike any key when ready''
          ..then insert the MSDOS System Disk.

When you see the message:
 ''Insert diskette for drive A: and strike any key when ready''
          ..then insert the GEM Startup Disk.
****************************************************************
Insert diskette for drive B: and strike
any key when ready
```

You now remove your GEM disk, put the MS-DOS disk into the drive and press, rather than 'strike', the <ENTER>, or any other, key. The green drive lights will come on briefly and then the additional prompt appears on the display:

```
Insert diskette for drive A: and strike
any key when ready
```

At this stage you remove the MS-DOS disk and place your GEM disk back into the drive. Now when you press a key the whole screen briefly clears and the same display appears as before, explaining what you have to do and requesting that you 'insert diskette for drive B.' This does rather give the impression that something has gone wrong. For a moment you fear that you are going to be involved in a continuous loop. In fact it is simply a rather clumsy way of making sure that the explanation about which disk should be placed in the drive each time remains permanently on the screen.

Placing the MS-DOS disk in the drive and pressing a key soon brings up the further request for the GEM disk. This time, as you press a key and the display recycles, there is a briefly visible screen message about 'installing' the mouse. This is rather reassuring because it confirms that something different is happening.

The third time you swap MS-DOS and GEM disks, a new prompt appears at the bottom of the screen and remains there for a while. This states that the computer is:

```
Loading GEM. Please wait....
```

After a slight delay the screen begins to become quite interesting. An elegant 'GEM' in larger typeface is placed on the centre of the display, followed shortly after by the GEM desktop display, with small pictures, the GEM Icons, distributed over the two halves of the screen.

Returning to GEM

This initial encounter with GEM will not be repeated in exactly this guise unless you subsequently reinstall it from your initial disk on to another back-up floppy.

The next time when you run GEM you will begin with the MS-DOS A-prompt again, and type GEM <ENTER>. The display will now be the much briefer:

```
A>GEM

-- Installing Mouse Device Driver V5.00b --

Loading GEM, Please wait ...
```

This is all you have to do. There is no sequence of repeated disk swapping, involving your MS-DOS disk as before. This can therefore be put safely back into your disk box until the next time you switch on the Sinclair PC, or specifically require MS-DOS for some reason. After a pause, GEM Desktop appears.

The initial GEM desktop

At first GEM Desktop does not seem to be as user friendly as you might have expected. One of the problems with GEM is that the graphics potential of an unexpanded IBM PC-compatible computer is not really adequate to produce icons which are easily recognised. You might possibly regard this as being an unpromising beginning for a user interface dedicated to making everything as simple as possible.

GEM's solution is to label its icons and describe, albeit briefly, what each means. In the top half of the screen, with the overall description GEMAPPS (for applications) are the names:

```
New Folder
FONTS
GEMSYS
DOODLE.APP
OUTPUT.APP
PAINT.APP
OUTPUT.INF
DOODLE.RSC
OUTPUT.RSC
PAINT.RSC
```

In the separate, lower rectangle of the GEM Desktop there will be the additional icon labelled:

```
FLOPPY DISK
```

For your initial GEM experience do not worry about any of these except the icon marked DOODLE.APP. This is by far the easiest and most user friendly for the GEM novice.

A first GEM exercise - DR DOODLE

The somewhat daunting appearance of the GEM worktop when you see it for the first time is softened by the inclusion of a very simple art package written by Digital Research. This is their DOODLE application, a modestly titled piece of software which slightly resembles the familiar children's drawing toy. Just as with suitable twirls of the two buttons on the bottom of the toy a thin line will trace shakily across a plastic screen, so the DOODLE screen will faithfully recreate the passage of the Sinclair PC's mouse over its table top. Also like the toy, it is not very easy at first to produce a realistic picture. Hence the name 'doodle'. Although with practice you might begin to draw something you do feel proud of, it is better to regard this particular GEM application as useful practice in learning your way about GEM desktop and acquiring some of the techniques you are going to need for serious work later.

Selecting a GEM application - clicking the mouse

You begin the DOODLE application by first using the mouse to move the screen pointer into the icon marked DOODLE.APP. Then you have to click the left hand button on the mouse twice in rapid succession. Clicking only once will only highlight the icon and not actually begin the application.

Briefly the hour glass icon appears at the centre of the display. This is GEM's rather unfortunate equivalent of the 'Please wait' screen message which other software usually provides while data is being read from a disk. It is hard to understand why a slightly more encouraging icon was not devised, perhaps an athlete sprinting, or a stop watch. Fortunately you do not need to wait an hour before DOODLE is ready. Worry about those applications where a cup of coffee icon might be appropriate.

If you move the mouse around your adjacent flat surface while the hour glass is on the screen, it will move too. This does give you something with which you can amuse yourself should the delay prove frustrating!

Avoiding trouble with the menu bar

There is a great deal crammed on to the GEM desktop. It is rather like wandering round one of those rather more cramped and over-ambitious department stores which insist upon putting the display of cut glass immediately next to the duvets. You creep about, wondering what you will stagger into next.

The chances are that you will already, in your attempt to select the DOODLE application, have encountered the GEM 'menu bar'. This is the band across the top of the screen with the words: **Files**, **Options**, **Arrange** and **DESKTOP**. Each of these will display a little table of contents if you brush against it with your pointer. Each of these is a 'menu'. For example **Files** will add a display like this:

```
Open
Info/Rename..    I
*****************
Delete...         D
Format...
*****************
To output        ^U
Exit to DOS      ^Q
```

The **Options** menu is:

```
Install disk drive...
Configure application...   A
************************
Set preferences...
Save desktop              V
Enter DOS commands        C
```

Arrange has the menu:

```
Show as text       S
******************
Sort by name       N
Sort by type       P
Sort by size       Z
Sort by date       T
```

Finally, **DESKTOP** will display:

```
Desktop info...
*******************
Snapshot
Calculator
Clock
Print Spooler
```

These are the menus available before DOODLE has loaded. Once that is operating they will not be the same. If such a menu is obscuring the screen while you are trying to find the DOODLE icon the solution is quite simple. Move the pointer to a free area of the screen, away from any icons, and click the mouse. The screen will immediately return to the original desktop in a most satisfying way. It is rather like opening a convenient drawer on a real desk and quickly sweeping everything inside. A more accurate analogy would be with the wastepaper basket, because GEM retains no memory of what you have just done.

Erasing your picture

The initial DOODLE 'window' is a rectangular area occupying the top left-hand quarter of the screen. The menu bar is still present at the top of the screen, but beneath this is the title of this particular application:

```
DR DOODLE for the Sinclair PC200
```

When you move the pointer with the mouse about the screen, it is not confined to this window. You can also move across the background area occupying the remaining three quarters of the display. There is one immediate difference, however. If you click the mouse when the pointer is in a particular position on the screen, it will leave a small cross to mark this position only if it is in the window. This distinguishes between the active part of the display and the rest.

Holding the left-hand button down on the mouse as the pointer is moved across the window will leave a continuous line behind it. In this way you can start to build up your first doodle. It is likely, of course, that you will not be too satisfied with this first attempt. To remove what you have done so far, place the pointer on the **Options** part of the menu bar. You do not need to click the mouse. The word **Options** is then highlighted and beneath it is a different choice from the Options menu shown before:

```
Pen / Eraser Selection...
Erase Picture
```

This new menu will be obscuring a small portion of your artistic creation, but do not worry. Moving the pointer back on to any part of the window itself and clicking the mouse once will restore things to the way before. Your picture reappears.

If however you move the pointer about on the menu itself you will highlight in turn either **Pen / Eraser Selection** or **Erase Picture**. You wish to forget quickly your first effort with DOODLE and so you click the mouse while the appropriate choice is highlighted. Both your picture, and the menu, then disappear, leaving you with the DOODLE window just as it was when you began.

Experimenting with window size - 'dragging'

The initial DOODLE window is not very large and you will soon want to make it bigger. There is a particular GEM technique for doing this which reappears in different situations throughout the operation of the GEM environment. This is the process of 'dragging'.

Place the pointer on the small square which is located at the bottom right-hand side of the window. It is then important that you hold the button down on the mouse the whole time. If you do this, as you move the pointer around the screen an image of the current DOODLE window will follow it. This continues until you release the button. The window is then altered in size and shape to the new rectangle you have selected. This method can be used to make the window either bigger or smaller.

Note that there is a minimum window size which DOODLE will allow you to select. You cannot make the window smaller than the final square achieved by dragging the bottom right-hand corner as far as you can towards the top left. At this point the window's ghostly outline breaks free from the influence of the pointer.

If you want the DOODLE window the same size as the whole screen, there is a quicker method. Move the pointer to the small box at the top of the right-hand side. Click the mouse once. The window will now fill the entire screen. Clicking on the box again returns to the smaller window.

Choosing the media

Once you have decided upon the size your picture is going to be, you will need to select the type of 'pen' you will use for it. To do this, take the pointer to **Options** on the menu bar and click the mouse. This time, click again on the **Pen / Eraser** choice. When you do this, your picture will have superimposed a GEM dialogue box. The accompanying text is:

```
Doodle Pen / Eraser Selection

Pens:                          Ok
Erasers:                       Cancel
```

This box provides you with a choice of three different sized pens and three equivalent erasers, also of graded width. The selection is not really over-generous. A similar DOODLE application provided with GEM on the Amstrad 1512 also comes with a selection of different screen colours. Nevertheless, this Sinclair version of DOODLE does provide sufficient facilities for you to familiarise yourself with GEM before attempting more serious work.

As you move the pointer towards one of the six choices, a small outline will jump to the relevant part of the window to emphasise the selection you are about to make. However your choice is not finalised until you click the pointer on the **Ok** box. The window will then disappear completely, returning you to the DOODLE window you had before. You can now begin your drawing with the type of pen you have selected. When you wish to alter the thickness of the line you are drawing, use **Options** again to return to the pen selection window. Obviously at first there is no point in choosing one of the erasers. These do become useful once you have begun drawing a picture, though, because you can create quite interesting effects by deleting areas of black already on the DOODLE window.

Changing your mind

While looking at the choice of pens and erasers, you may decide that you prefer instead to remain with your current choice. This means that none of the six possibilities are relevant and that you wish to return immediately to the DOODLE window, without the extra pen selection box blocking your view. If this is the case, move the pointer to the **Cancel** box and click. The original picture then returns, unaffected by what has just taken place.

The **Ok/Cancel** choice is a common feature of GEM throughout its many applications. The general rule to follow is simple. When you are certain that you have made the correct choice within the box, click on **Ok**. Alternatively, if you want to return to the previous display without any further additions or alterations, click on **Cancel.**

Drawing your picture

Remember that the process of drawing your picture is very much like dragging the bottom right-hand corner of the window. If you want to produce a continuous line, hold the button down as you move the mouse. If you want to jump to a different part of the picture without leaving a line behind, slide the pointer across without depressing the button. The simplicity of this, combined with the choice of pens and erasers, will allow you to create your picture. Initially you may find that the mouse control is a little difficult, but it is mainly a question of practice. Mistakes can always be removed by an appropriate eraser.

Modifying a picture

Instead of creating a picture of your own, you might decide to look at the one already provided with the DOODLE application. This is a picture of a tiger. Once loaded from the GEM back-up disk, it can always be modified by erasing parts of it and drawing your own details on top. Plagiarism is extremely easy! An exercise like this is useful practice in controlling the mouse and working with the menu bar. Remember, of course, that the original picture is still present upon the disk.

To obtain the tiger picture, take the pointer to **Files** on the menu bar. As you should already be within the DOODLES application, the Files menu will again be different from the original list given above, just as it was for Options. Now you will see:

```
Load
Save
Save As...
Abandon
Quit
```

As you move the pointer down through this menu you will notice something different happening compared with similar operations you have already carried out. Not all the choices will be highlighted as the pointer passes over them. GEM is sensibly error trapped to prevent your choosing inappropriate parts of the menu. Only the three choices: **Load, Save As...** and **Quit** will show that they are available to you by becoming highlighted. This is also pointed out to you by the fact that these words appear in a heavier typeface on the menu when it is first selected from the menu bar. You wish to see the tiger picture and so you click on the choice **Load**.

An early encounter with MS-DOS

At this stage, GEM unfortunately loses some of its user friendliness! You must remember, of course, that the purpose of GEM is mainly to protect you from the rigours of the MS-DOS operating system. Although GEM provides homely pictures and carefully error-trapped menus and alternatives, MS-DOS is lurking in the background the whole time. Sometimes it will claw its way through GEM's chatty screen display and a piece of pure operating system terminology will appear on the display. Cynics might suggest that this rather defeats the whole purpose of GEM. The sensible attitude is probably to accept that, in life generally, the horror of reality is inevitable sometimes, but can usually be ignored. Now is not such an occasion. The new box which has been superimposed upon your picture is no longer the readily comprehended GEM type of display so far encountered. Neatly tabulated, within a typical GEM format are the following expressions:

```
ITEM SELECTOR

Directory: A:\IMAGES\*.IMG_____

     *.IMG                    Selection: _____.___

   TIGER .IMG
```

Here you are being exposed to various MS-DOS concepts simultaneously. As a technical aside, these are filenames, filename extensions, pathnames and wildcards. All of these will be explained in the MS-DOS section of this book. For the present try to regard this as superfluous screen decoration which need not concern you further.

You will also see the familiar choice of **OK** or **Cancel** which faithfully accompanies GEM displays. If you lose heart and click the mouse when the pointer is placed on the **Cancel** box you will immediately return to your picture exactly as it was before. To display the tiger, all you need do is click the mouse on the word 'TIGER'. It will become highlighted, but nothing else will happen until you shift the pointer to **OK** and click again. A picture of a tiger be loaded from the disk and replace the existing display.

Creative artist or vandal?

The amount of the tiger which will appear depends upon the size of the DOODLE window selected. To see all of it, click on the 'full-size' box at the top right-hand corner.

After that, appropriate use of the three pens and erasers available via the options menu will allow you to modify the tiger as much as you like. Take care at first. Until you have become expert with the small movements needed for full mouse control, it is fairly easy to erase more of the tiger than you intend. There is no ready 'restore' option to which you can resort and replace details removed by mistake.

However, the non-artist will be relieved to know that it is extremely easy to convert the tiger into quite a convincing giant panda. Wait till that point before letting friends into the room to see what you have done.

Saving a sketch

When you are satisfied with the picture you have drawn with DOODLE, you may wish to save it permanently on disk so that later you can admire it again. You might also want to save an unfinished masterpiece to be completed later during your next GEM session. GEM allows you to record your work quite easily.

First you have to move the desktop pointer to the word **Files** in the menu bar. Within the DOODLES application, the menu will again be different from the list given above, just as it was for **Options** Now you will see the menu:

```
Load
Save
Save As...
Abandon
Quit
```

As you move the pointer down through this menu you will notice that not all the choices will be highlighted as the pointer passes them. Only the three choices on the menu appear in heavier typeface: **Load, Save As..** and **Quit,** and are available to by becoming highlighted. GEM is therefore forcing you to save your picture under a specific name. You click the mouse on the choice **Save As...**The item selector appears again, now allowing you to choose a name for the sketch. Type this in and click on **OK** to transfer your creation to disk.

4

Exploring GEM further

Experimenting with DOODLE will give you the confidence to investigate GEM in greater depth. The essential point to remember is that GEM has been designed to make an IBM PC-compatible machine like the Sinclair PC as user friendly as possible. The mouse and pointer are employed to avoid the difficulty of typing at the keyboard, and the icons on the screen used to identify the different operations easily, without placing a barrier between computer and the person operating it.

It might be argued by some that the true solution to such a problem is simply to encourage people to learn at least a few typing skills in the first place, and to acquire basic familiarity with computers and their operating systems. The latter is, of course, one of the objectives of the subsequent chapters of this book. The next generation of users will have progressed through schools equipped with microcomputers. They will employ these to help with general studies and have specific lessons in computing. They may regard GEM with a degree of amusement. It might then seem to be a needless anachronism dating from a naïve past. For the present, however, GEM undoubtedly has a justified role of making computers more presentable through analogy with familiar objects. An example of this is the Desktop menu which refers to everyday office items, like a calculator or clock.

The desk accessories

Taking the pointer to the extreme right of the menu bar will yield this menu:

```
Desktop info...
********************
Snapshot
Calculator
Clock
Print spooler
```

Each of these can be highlighted in turn. Clicking on the first one gives you a title screen only telling you the version of GEM you have, plus various incidental details. It also states the names of the authors, Michael Franusich and Lowell Webster. (The philosophically literate will be excited by the copyright date given. This is exactly one year short of the centenary of the famous Austrian philosopher, Ludwig Wittgenstein, who was born on April 26th 1889. Sadly it is less exciting for him because he died just after his sixty second birthday and thus missed the opportunity to contribute to the new field of philosophy of computing.)

To return to the menu, you must click on the **OK** box to remove this information window. The other accessories, the calculator and clock are described below.

Using the desktop calculator

If you click the mouse on **Calculator** on the menu, the display will be temporarily overwritten by a picture of a realistic looking calculator, complete with keys and apparent LCD display. Just in case you still unable to recognise it, the name 'Calculator' is shown as well.

There are two ways in which you can perform some arithmetic with this calculator. Whichever you choose, the answer will appear on the calculator's display, just like the real thing.

The first method is to use the mouse to move the pointer over the calculator's keyboard, clicking on the digits you require. You must watch the display carefully to make sure that you have pressed the mouse's button sufficiently firmly so that the digits do appear. When you select one of the functions, this will not be shown on the display, of course. Real calculators do not usually show arithmetical signs either. Clicking on the equals sign will then display the answer.

The calculator has a memory function. You can add or subtract current numbers in the display to the memory or from it. Previously stored values can be recalled when required. Naturally the memory, as well as the display, can be cleared.

The alternative way to operate the calculator is to use the keypad on the right-hand side of the Sinclair PC's keyboard. Numbers and some functions can be entered directly from here. Results of calculations will be shown on the calculator's display as before.

When you have finished using the calculator, click on the 'close' box icon to the left of the word 'Calculator' and the calculator will disappear. The screen display will return exactly to the original shown before you used the facility.

Adjusting the clock

Clicking on the word **Clock** on the desktop menu will place a small digital display on the left-hand side of the screen. This shows the time according to a twenty four hour format and beneath this the date. These can all can be adjusted if necessary using a combination of mouse and keyboard.

Try taking the pointer to the hours figure and clicking the mouse. The number will be highlighted. Now type in the correct, two digit value for the hour. The highlighting will be replaced with the new hour figure. Do precisely the same for the minutes.

The date is altered in the same way. Click on the day of the month and type in the appropriate number. You may encounter an apparent difficulty with the month. Although this is shown by a single digit, it must be typed in as two. This means that you should enter 01 for January, 02 for February etc. If you do not realise this, and perhaps type a 2 twice, thinking that the first time you failed to press the key heavily enough, GEM will imagine that you are attempting to specify the twenty second month of the year. It then beeps, to indicate your error. Obviously, a combination of any two numbers will be accepted for the year.

Setting an alarm

It is often useful when you are working to set an alarm in the background to remind you when you ought to be doing something else. The GEM clock provides this facility.

To the left of the time display is an extremely small clock icon. This shows that the clock has not currently been set with an alarm. If you click on the icon it will change shape to a more recognisable bell. You can now set the hour and minutes figure just as before by clicking and typing. Finally you click on the note icon to the right of the time display. When this is highlighted, the alarm is set. You can turn off the alarm by clicking once more on the icon and making it dim again.

The alarm sounds as a rapid series of five beeps. With the Sinclair PC's volume control adjusted to maximum this is loud enough to distract you even if you have moved to another part of the room.

Once the alarm has been set it will sound at the specified time even when you have begun doing something else entirely. It really does prove to be a small, but extremely useful, additional aid to your work. Computers can become very time consuming, letting you forget just how late it is in the evening!

Housekeeping with a computer

The floppy disks which the Sinclair PC uses to store its data can hold a great deal of information relating to the various applications for which you employ the machine. Soon you will need to consider a sensible way of organising your material. Fortunately the analogy with an ordinary office environment is preserved and GEM refers to the 'folders' in which your files may be kept.

GEM assumes that you will be systematic in the way you remember where various items are stored and encourages you to imagine that you really do have a virtual office tucked away inside the Sinclair PC. Different documents and files will be placed carefully into appropriately named folders and these themselves might be located inside yet another folder which encompasses the subject material of all the folders it contains.

Obviously in order to use such a system successfully, you will need to be able to create folders of your own.

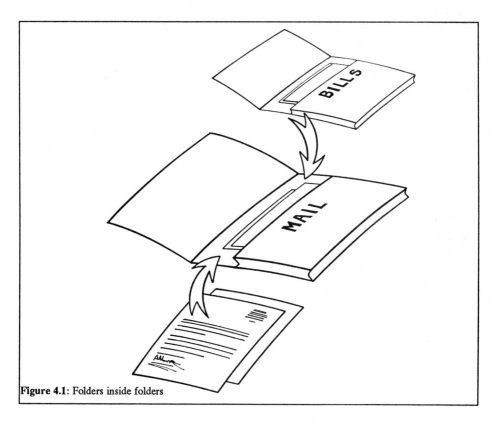

Figure 4.1: Folders inside folders

Creating a new folder

Suppose that you wish to create a new folder to store your DOODLE picture. First you need to work back through the various levels of the directory structure until you display the relevant set of icons . Click on the 'close' box at the top left-hand corner of the window to work back through the various levels. The final stage you can encounter will show just the floppy disk icon with the 'directory path' normally displayed at the top of the screen, replaced by 'Disk drives:'. This means that you have gone back too far. Double click on the disk icon to proceed to the next level of the directory. You will now see the folder titled 'IMAGES'.

Double click on this icon to open the IMAGES folder. Now, to create a new folder within this one, you need to double click on the new folder icon. A dialogue box then appears:

```
NEW FOLDER

Name: _____ . ____

     OK        Cancel
```

Choose a suitable name for your new folder. Convention suggests that a folder name should not use the optional three character extension. This allows a ready distinction to be observed between folder names and file names. Suppose that you type in the folder name POLLOCK. This is in memory of the American artist Jackson Pollock, who invented a distinctive 'drip technique'. (You are, remember, intending to use the folder for your GEM DOODLE creations!):

```
NEW FOLDER

Name: POLLOCK_ . ____

     OK        Cancel
```

After this, click on **OK**. The Sinclair PC's disk drive will activate briefly and then the screen display will be updated to show the new folder, POLLOCK.

As a further exercise, you could now follow the same steps as detailed above to create yet another folder within the IMAGES folder. First click on the 'close' box, then double click on the new folder icon. The same dialogue box will appear. This time, perhaps the name of another twentieth century artist could be selected:

```
NEW FOLDER

Name: ERNST____ . ____

     OK        Cancel
```

You now click on **OK**, as before. A folder with the name 'ERNST' is added to the screen icons.

Exploring directory paths

If at this stage you double click on the ERNST icon, the title bar of the display will show:

```
A:\IMAGES\ERNST\
```

This is the directory path to your current position in the directory structure, which is the new folder created. The only icon that will be shown is the new folder icon. This is because nothing has been placed in the ERNST folder so far.

Now click on the 'close' box and you will move to the previous level of the directory structure. The directory path shown will be:

A:\IMAGES\

The new folder icon is accompanied by the ERNST folder, by POLLOCK, and by at least the TIGER file provided with GEM. Note the different shape used for this icon. At this point you could travel back down the structure into the POLLOCK folder by double clicking on the POLLOCK icon. The directory path shown will be:

A:\IMAGES\POLLOCK\

This is rather like an old vicarage where you might travel from the kitchen to the study by first going up the back staircase to the landing, then down the main stairs again.

Alternatively you might decide to go further back through the structure and again click on the 'close' box. The level of the directory reached will now be shown by the directory path:

A:\

This is the root directory. Amongst the many icons now on display will the IMAGES folder from which you have just made your exit and in which the POLLOCK and ERNST folders are contained. By double clicking on suitable icons at this level, you can explore the directory structure further.

Copying a folder

You may continue the analogy with cardboard and paper further by electing to place your ERNST folder inside POLLOCK. Your first step is to make sure that you are at the correct level of the directory structure. By now you should be sufficiently practised in this to reach the right level quickly. You either open an appropriate icon by double clicking on it or, alternatively, work in the opposite direction through the directory structure by clicking once on the 'close' box. You will know that you have arrived at the correct level when you see as your directory path:

A:\IMAGES\

Both the ERNST and POLLOCK icons will be present on the screen.

To place the first folder inside the second one, move the pointer on to the ERNST icon. Click and hold the mouse button down and then drag towards the POLLOCK icon. A GEM hand icon will appear. Position this over the POLLOCK icon before releasing the button. This dialogue box will then be seen:

COPY FOLDERS / ITEMS

Folders to copy: __1
Items to copy: __0

OK   Cancel

Click on **OK**. ERNST is now a folder inside the POLLOCK folder. You can check this easily by tracing through the directory paths. First double click on the POLLOCK icon. The directory path shown will be:

$$A:\backslash IMAGES\backslash POLLOCK\backslash$$

In addition to the new folder icon, the ERNST icon will also be displayed. Double clicking on this will give the directory path:

$$A:\backslash IMAGES\backslash POLLOCK\backslash ERNST\backslash$$

Only the new folder icon will now be seen.

Examining a folder's contents

You may decide that you want to check the content of a folder that you have created. To do this you will first need to display its icon on the screen. Then click on the icon and drag towards the word **File** on the menu bar. The GEM hand icon will appear as you do this. Release the button only when you arrive at the correct part of the menu bar. The Files menu is now displayed:

```
Open
Info/Rename...

* * * * * * * * * * * * * * * * * * * * *
Delete
Format
To Output
Exit to DOS
```

As you take the pointer down the menu, **Info/Rename** can be highlighted. Click here.

```
FOLDER INFORMATION

          Folder name:   ERNST____.____
              Created:        13-01-89      09:47 am
   Number of folders:            0
     Number of items:            0
           Bytes used:            0

                                              OK
```

When you have seen what is present, you simply click on **OK** to return to the previous display.

Listing all your files and folders

GEM allows you to check all of your files and folders in detail. This is achieved with the **Arrange** menu. When you take your pointer to this word on the menu bar you will see this added to your display:

```
        Show as text        S

        *******************
        Sort by name        N
        Sort by type        P
        Sort by size        Z
        Sort by date        T
```

In the following, it will be assumed that the current directory path is :

```
        A:\IMAGES\.
```

By clicking on the first item of this menu - Show as text - you can replace the icons with a text description of the IMAGES folder. This gives the names of files and folders present, the date and time of their creation and also the size in bytes of the files:

```
        New folder          00-00-80    12:00 am
        POLLOCK             13-01-89    09:34 am
        ERNST               13-01-89    09:47 am
        TIGER  GEM       94 11-08-88    01:52 pm
        TIGER  IMG     6680 11-08-88    01:52 pm
```

The **Arrange** menu has altered, and now indicates:

```
        Show as icons       S

        *******************
        Sort by name        N
        Sort by type        P
        Sort by size        Z
        Sort by date        T
```

When a large number of items are present, searching for one specific file is made easier using by the sorting facilities available. For example, clicking on the second option on the menu leads to the alphabetical arrangement:

```
        New folder          00-00-80    12:00 am
        ERNST                           09:47 am
        POLLOCK             13-01-89    09:34 am
        TIGER GEM        94 11-08-88    01:52 pm
        TIGER  IMG     6680 11-08-88    01:52 pm
```

Sometimes it is easier to locate a particular item by sorting according to the date, assuming that you can remember roughly when you worked on the file or folder in question.

Changing a file's name

If you want to change the name of a file you must first make sure that its icon is displayed on the screen. Click on the icon and drag to **Files**. On the menu which appears, **Info/Rename** will be highlighted. If you click here you will see:

```
ITEM INFORMATION / RENAME


        Name:   TIGER .IMG
   Size in bytes:    ____6680
   Last modified:  11/08/88 01:52 pm
        Attributes: Read/Write Read-Only
                        OK      Cancel
```

Type in the new name for the file:

```
ITEM INFORMATION / RENAME


        Name: PUSSY .CAT
   Size in bytes: ____6680
   Last modified: 11/08/88 01:52 pm
        Attributes: Read/Write Read-Only
                        OK      Cancel
```

Now click on **OK**. The same icons appear as before, except the one selected has the new name.

Changing a folder's name

The method required for renaming a folder is more complicated. First you must set up a new folder with the name you require. Then copy the contents of the original folder across, using the method described earlier. Finally delete the first folder using the procedure outlined below.

Removing a file or folder

You can remove a file or folder quite easily. Click on the appropriate icon and drag it to **Files** on the menu bar. Release the button and the menu will appear. Now click on **Delete**. If you have selected a folder you will see:

```
DELETE FOLDERS / ITEMS

Folders to delete: ____1
   Items to delete: ___0


     OK      Cancel
```

Clicking on **OK** completes the process. Deleting folders and files is a good opportunity to practice the mouse technique of dragging more than one icon at once. For example, you might now decide to kill off both ERNST and POLLOCK. Form a rectangle by clicking at the top left of their mutual position on the screen and dragging the rectangular outline down towards the bottom right. Continue till both are enclosed. Then release the button. Take the pointer to **Files** and click on **Delete** when the menu appears. This time you will see:

```
DELETE FOLDERS / ITEMS

Folders to delete: ___3
  Items to delete: ___0

     OK     Cancel
```

Remember that ERNST was placed in POLLOCK, hence the total.

5

Investigating GEM Paint

Depending on how you intend to use your Sinclair PC, you may buy many application programs which can be accessed from GEM desktop. However your initial familiarity with GEM will probably come through using GEM Paint, because this application is bundled with the machine.

It is also an extremely pleasant way of becoming adept at using your Sinclair PC. Although it is a serious application, GEM Paint has many of attributes of a good quality game! It is certainly an absorbing way of spending an evening, as well as a tool which allows you to do some serious work.

Making room for a picture

Before you begin a particular GEM Paint session, you should make sure that you have room on your GEM back-up disk for any pictures that you will wish to save later. It is quite possible that unnecessary work has been retained from, perhaps, an earlier exploration of DOODLE. This should be removed now to avoid any trouble when you come to leave GEM Paint.

First, you will need to explore the disk file structure, so that you can establish whether any space on the disk is being wasted.

The easiest way of doing this is to keep clicking the mouse on the 'close' box at the top left-hand corner of the screen until you have gone as far back in the structure as you can. Now, at its highest level, you will just see the floppy disk icon in the upper window. The lower half of the screen will not have changed.

Move the pointer to the floppy disk icon and double click the mouse button. The title bar will display A:\ and the relevant set of icons will appear. Choose the icon which has IMAGES printed beneath it and double click the mouse button again. The previous display will be replaced with A:\IMAGES\ in the title bar and icons representing any work which has been saved from DOODLE. If you have been using GEM Paint already there might be other named icons as well. Decide now which of these icons should be removed and delete them in the way described in the previous chapter. There is no reason why you should not abandon the TIGER folder as well. You are working with your GEM back-up disk and the TIGER folder will still be present on your original GEM disk, should you wish to use it again later. At this stage you might delete all the files and end simply with the new folder icon.

Now click on the 'close' box to return to the root directory of the disk. The title bar will display this as **A:** again.

Selecting GEM Paint

GEM Paint is not directly available from the root directory. You must move the pointer to the GEMAPPS icon and double click the mouse button. The title bar now shows **A:\GEMAPPS** Move the pointer to the icon marked PAINT.APP and double click once more. GEM desktop will now be abandoned. The hour glass appears on the screen while GEM Paint loads from the disk. **A:\GEMAPPS\PAINT.APP** is displayed temporarily at the top of the screen and then you will see the GEM Paint display. This consists of a 'paint window' at the centre of the screen, two broad rectangles either side forming the 'tools' and 'paint' palette and the menu bar at the top.

The menu bar

As you move the pointer across the menu bar, you will see the seven possible menus which can be selected. For example, the File menu includes:

```
            New
            Open

        **************
            Close
            Save
            Save As . . .
            Abandon

        **************
            To Output . . .
            Quit
```

Momentarily overwriting the screen in a similar way, the Tools menu shows:

```
            Undo (Esc)

        ****************
            Grid On
            Transparent On

        ****************
            Brush shape
            View Picture
            Size Picture
```

Initially, there is no need to concern yourself too much with the content of these menus. There is a great deal to learn in GEM Paint and it is best to proceed slowly at first. Do not worry too much about all the details. It will probably take several sessions working with GEM Paint before you have mastered all possibilities.

Adjusting the Paint window

You can alter the dimensions of your Paint window using the usual GEM technique of dragging. Place the pointer on the 'size' box in the lower right-hand corner. Hold the mouse button down and slide the pointer up, and to the left, until you have the size and shape that you require. Then release the button. As with the DOODLE application, the window will reform along the new boundary that you have defined.

If you wish to return to the original window size, click on the 'full-size' box at the top right-hand corner. The window then reappears as in the initial display. Clicking once more on the 'full-size' box will take you back to the smaller window previously chosen.

Once you have decided upon the dimensions you require for your window, you can move it to a new position on the screen. Slide the pointer to the title bar. Perversely this will be initially identified by the single word 'untitled'. Click the mouse and hold the button down as you drag the title bar to a fresh location on the screen. Releasing the button will then place the paint window at this new site. You can behave like an impatient artist who cannot quite decide where to place the easel.

The GEM paint palette

As already mentioned, your paint window has two vertical rectangles, one on either side. These are the palettes which allow you to choose the way in which your create the picture.

The right-hand rectangle is the pattern palette. It is designed very much like a mathematical model of a real palette of paints that an artist might use. A colour from one of the selection on an artist's palette is usually transferred to a mixing and testing area before being applied to canvas. GEM Paint operates in a similar way. The pattern chosen will be displayed in the top rectangle before you begin using it.

You will notice as you propel the cursor across the screen with the mouse, that it adopts its conventional pointer shape only when superimposed on a palette. When it is on the actual painting area itself it will appear in a number of different guises. Often you will see a small black square.

Practice using the right-hand palette now. Position the pointer over one of the twenty-seven small squares which display your choice of possible pattern. Click the mouse once and the effect you have chosen will appear in the larger top rectangle. You can repeat this as many times as you like before moving the pointer to the paint window itself. Hold the button down as you move the mouse and you will see the black square followed by a swathe of the pattern you have adopted. Releasing the button allows you to move the position for the next piece of pattern.

Changing the pattern a few times will let you build up an interesting abstract picture but does not really make it possible to create anything more satisfying. Before going on to explore what else GEM Paint offers, you will need to clear the window and start again.

Beginning a fresh picture

You can clear the window by taking the pointer to **Files** on the menu bar. The files menu reappears. You have apparently the same choice as before: **New, Open, Close, Save, Save As..., Abandon, To Output** and **Quit**, but this time the choice **Abandon** can be highlighted. Before, when there was no picture present, this choice was not a relevant. Now you can click the mouse on this word to display a dialogue box with a large question mark accompanied by the additional text:

```
Abandon edited image?   Abandon
                          Save
                         Cancel
```

At this stage, all you want to do is remove your picture so that you can explore other GEM Paint techniques. Just click on **Abandon** and both the dialogue box and your picture disappear.

An alternative and faster way of clearing the paint window is explained below in the section on the GEM Paint eraser.

The GEM tools palette

On the left-hand side of the GEM Paint window is the tools palette. There is a great deal to investigate here. The top half of the tools palette consists of fifteen small squares, each of which illustrates a possible tool you may wish to use as you create a picture. The painting tools are represented by quite detailed icons that show fairly clearly their intended effect.

Beginning at the top left-hand corner of the tools palette, the individual choices are the microscope, selector (or window), text, pencil, eraser, straight line, paint brush, paint sprayer, paint tap, rectangle, rounded box, polygon, arc, circle and free form. (The terms used here are not quite the same as those employed in the manual but do agree with the standard names used, for example, in the book on GEM Paint by Stephen Morris.)

Experiment with selecting a particular tool by moving the pointer over the fifteen squares. If you click the mouse on one of them, the appropriate tool will be highlighted. However at this stage you must be careful. Do not move back into the paint window yet because it is best not to investigate the tools in the order in which they are presented. They vary in their complexity. The microscope, for example, is a rather subtle device and capable of giving you great control over the detail in your picture, once you have drawn the rough outline. Thus it would be an inappropriate choice to begin with. Instead, it would be better to start by learning to use the pencil.

Drawing lines with the pencil

This tool allows you to build up your initial outline. First click the mouse on the pencil in the tools palette. This is the left-hand icon in the second row down. When you move the pointer across the paint window it will now appear as a reasonably realistic pencil shape.

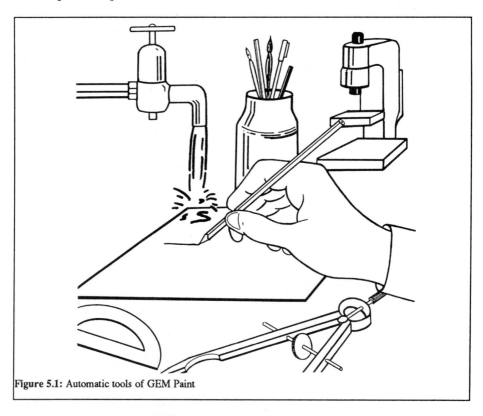

Figure 5.1: Automatic tools of GEM Paint

You will also need to choose the type of line that the pencil is going to draw. The 'colour' and thickness can both be adjusted. Immediately beneath the selection of tools is set of three horizontal rectangles. The first is narrow and just displays the current line colour. Under this are the two choices. Click on the one you require. The lower is the obvious first choice, since this will show on the initial blank screen, while the upper needs to be superimposed upon something dark. As you click the mouse on one of the choices, the narrow top rectangle will change to it, to indicate the one you have selected.

The thickness of the line is chosen on the panel beneath the colour choice. The left-hand side represents a slider to control the line width. Place the pointer on the slider and click the mouse. The horizontal bar on the slider will then jump to the position selected. At the same time a demonstration line appears on the right to show what will now be drawn when the pencil is moved to the paint window. A number is also displayed which calibrates the line width precisely, allowing you to fine tune the effects you produce.

In addition to jumping the slider to a chosen position, you can also drag it up and down in the usual GEM fashion.

Once you are satisfied with the line type, move to the paint window and begin drawing. As before, holding the button down as you move the mouse will leave a continuous line. Releasing it permits you to go to another part of the window without drawing anything between the two points.

A little relaxation - the paint tap

As soon as you are competent in drawing lines, you can try using one of the more amusing, and potentially powerful, GEM Paint tools. This is the paint tap, which is selected by clicking on the right-hand icon in the third row from the top.

Care is needed when using the tap. To avoid unexpected effects, it is important first to make sure you have some totally enclosed areas drawn on the window using the pencil. Create some closed curves first. You may overlap these, like a set of loops scattered across the screen at random. The important point is that the curves are all completely joined. There must be no gaps which will allow the subsequent pattern to bleed through into the background area.

Once you have drawn the pattern that you are going to fill, return to the tools palette. Click the mouse on the paint tap to highlight it. Now move to the paint palette and click on the pattern you require. Check that it has been repeated at the top of the paint palette and then place the pointer inside one of the areas that you have chosen. Clicking will now fill the enclosed area in a very satisfying way with the pattern you have selected. By repeating the process you are able to create a complicated picture with various filled shapes.

While one of the shapes is being filled, you can stop the process if you click the mouse again. However, you do need to be very quick on the button. Reclicking on some part of the still unfilled area will continue the action of the paint tap.

Painting with the brush

The left-hand icon in the third row is the paint brush. Clicking once on this will allow you to create brush strokes which contrast with the pencil lines employed so far. If you only click once you will find yourself equipped with the current brush shape.

More interesting is to double click on the brush icon.

When you do this a dialogue box appears. This shows all the possible brush shapes from which you can choose, arranged in seven rows and five columns. The two columns on the left are for the 'paint sprayer' explained in a later section. The current brush shape is indicated by a rectangle enclosing it. Move the pointer to the brush you want to use and the rectangle will jump to this position. Make sure that this really is the brush you require before clicking the mouse because you will immediately return to your picture.

You can now continue with the picture you are producing. Just as the pencil was indicated by the pointer adopting the appropriate shape, so your selected brush shape will now appear at the pointer's position.

Adding a straight line

Return to the tools palette and click again on the pencil icon. However much practice you have acquired in controlling the mouse, you will probably find it very difficult to produce a perfectly straight line. Try it. Nevertheless, at some point you are going to require straight lines in the pictures you create.

GEM Paint allows you to draw straight lines very easily. You do not employ the standard pencil, however. Instead, click the mouse on the straight line icon. This is the right-hand square on the second row. When the icon is highlighted, move back to the paint window. The pointer will now be replaced by a crosshair. Decide where you want your straight line to begin and click the mouse on this position. After this, as you move about the window it will seem that a piece of taut elastic is following the pointer. You can stretch the line in any direction you like and control the length accordingly. When you have reached the point where you feel the line should terminate, click the mouse again. The line will now be frozen into this length and orientation.

Straight lines can be added indefinitely by this process. If you do change your mind about the last line added, press <Esc> at the top left of the keyboard.

Using the eraser

You are bound to make mistakes in your picture, but these can often be cured using the GEM Paint eraser. This is the middle icon on the second row.

You must be very careful when selecting this. Make sure that you only click once on the icon to highlight the eraser. If you double click, you will delete your entire picture. In fact, this is the quick way of removing a picture which no longer interests you. Should this happen by mistake, press <Esc> on the keyboard before you do anything else.

Once the eraser has been successfully highlighted you can remove parts of your picture by moving the pointer with the mouse button depressed.

Deleting selectively with the eraser

Fine alterations are possible with the eraser because its shape can be adjusted. First take the pointer to **Tools** on the menu bar and then click on the **Brush Shape...** option which appears on the menu. The dialogue box offering different brush shapes will be shown again. Click on an appropriate size and you will then be returned to your initial picture with an eraser suitable for the mistake you need to remove.

Returning to the previous picture

When you spoil a picture by inappropriate actions you can usually return to the previous stage reached, just by pressing <Esc>. Care is needed, however, because the 'previous stage' may often not be precisely as you remember it.

The paint sprayer

Added realism is provided in GEM Paint by the use of the paint sprayer. This allows areas of a picture to be filled with a less dense texture. It permits a more subtle, graded approach to certain subjects. The paint sprayer is the middle icon on the third row of the tools palette. Click the mouse here first. Then choose a shape from the tools menu, in the same way as previously explained for the brush itself. The same dialogue box will appear with seven rows and five columns. This time, as you are working with the sprayer and not a brush, you must restrict your choice to the two columns on the left. After choosing the shape you want here, go to the paint palette and select a pattern.

You can then begin to paint with the sprayer. The difference between this and the brush is immediately obvious. A fine pattern will be built up, consisting of small dots on the screen. Just as with a real paint spray or artist's air brush, you can attempt to create a sense of texture and shading . Respraying a particular area will emphasise the effect.

More relaxation - copying with the selector

The paint tap allows you to complete a picture with the minimum of effort. A similar short cut is to copy parts of the picture and build up a finished work by repetition. Before you can do this you will need to complete a portion of the paint window with a sketch you feel is worth repeating. After this, click on the selector icon. This is the middle icon in the top row.

The pointer will assume the crosshair shape, as it did when you were drawing straight lines. Move it to the top left-hand corner of the area that you wish to copy. Now press <SHIFT> on the Sinclair PC's keyboard. Doing this will mean that the area you are going to select for copying will be a square. Two hands are necessary at this stage because you must keep <SHIFT> depressed while you hold the button down on the mouse as well. Move the crosshair diagonally down towards the bottom right of the area that you wish to copy. A square outline will grow from the initial position of the crosshair until it encloses the area you have selected. When you are satisfied that the correct part of the painting has been included, release <SHIFT> and the mouse button. The square outline will now begin to shimmer.

At this stage you can copy the content of the square to another part of the picture. Return the crosshair to inside the outline. It will change to a GEM hand icon. Holding the button down will let you drag the square outline to another part of the picture. When you release the button the original content of the square will reappear in the new box, leaving, of course, the original in its first position.

Before you repeat the process, press <SPACE> to fix this copy in position. You can then copy your second picture section to a third location in exactly the same way. Gradually a complicated picture can be constructed. A shimmering square is left around the last copy each time. When you wish to discontinue the process, click once on the eraser icon.

If you do not press <SPACE> after positioning the copy, GEM Paint will move the area you selected to the new position rather than creating an additional copy.

Moving part of the picture

You can move part of your painting in a very similar way. Follow the above sequence of operations up to the stage where you have an outline established for the area you wish to move. Return the crosshair to a position inside the outside and then depress the <CTRL> key on the keyboard. Hold the mouse button down and drag the outline to its new position. When you release <CTRL> and the button, the selected area will jump to the new location. No copy is created.

Further tricks with the selector

You are not restricted to a square shape for copying and moving parts of your picture. Rectangles are also possible. The first step in producing a rectangular area is to click on the selector icon as before and then move the crosshair to the top left-hand corner of your chosen picture detail. This time, do not hold down <SHIFT> as you click the mouse. Now you can drag a rectangular outline away from the corner and encompass the desired shape.

The most interesting effects with the selector are produced via the Selection menu. Again create a section of picture with which you wish to experiment and afterwards take the pointer to **Selection** on the menu bar. This menu appears again:

```
Clear
Complement
Flip Horizontal
Flip Vertical
```

You will have seen this already, when you first encountered GEM Paint. The difference before was that none of the choices could be highlighted. However now that you have already clicked on the selector icon in the tools palette, GEM Paint makes the selection menu accessible. All four choices are now available to you and any of them can be highlighted.

The first one lets you erase the content of the outline. Click the mouse on **Clear** and everything in the area you have selected will be erased. This erased area can be moved or copied in the same way as anything else.

The second choice, **Complement** switches all coloured areas from dark to light, and vice versa.

Dramatic effects are a possibility with the **Flip Horizontal** choice. Look carefully at the content of your square or rectangle first and watch what happens when you click on the option. It may be necessary here to create some special item of detail to emphasise the changes that take place. You will see that everything becomes laterally inverted, as if you have reflected the entire selected area in a vertical mirror. Clicking again on **Flip Horizontal** restores the original picture. This can be repeated indefinitely, toggling between one and the other version, until you make up your mind.

Clicking on the **Flip Vertical** option allows a similar inversion to take place, but this time the reflection appears vertically.

Of course, combinations of these various effects are all a possibility. You can alter something you have designed by reversing colours, horizontal and vertical orientation. A potentially useful technique is to keep two copies present on the screen and operate upon one of them only. Both may then be combined, by moving and copying, into a more advanced picture selection which itself could become the basis of further modification.

Placing a rectangle on your picture

The left-hand icon in the fourth row allows you to draw rectangles in to your picture. As you plan your rectangle, you should work through a list of options in the following way:

First click on the rectangle icon. Next click on the line colour, from the choice beneath the tools icons. After this, the line width is chosen with the slider, just as it was for drawing simple lines. Then select the pattern you want to use from the paint palette.

After you have completed these choices, move the pointer to the picture area. It becomes a crosshair again. Decide where you want your rectangle to begin and depress the button on the mouse. Your rectangle is then constructed by dragging outwards and releasing the button when you have the required shape. Further rectangles can then be added with the same line colour and width and pattern, simply by clicking the mouse on a new location and dragging again. Of course you can alter some, or all, of the rectangle's properties by going through the above routine again.

The rounded box

A different shape you may wish to add is the rounded box. This is the icon next to the rectangle in the fourth row. Click on it and carry out the steps detailed above for line colour, thickness and the pattern with which the rounded box will be filled. After this, choose the location for the rounded box and drag it to the required size.

If you wish to draw a rounded box which has sides of equal length, hold down <SHIFT> while you are dragging the box to size.

Ambitious shapes with the polygon

GEM Paint gives you the opportunity to design polygonal shapes of your own. You are not restricted to any given number of vertices. As with the other shapes you can generate, you can select the line width and colour as well as the fill pattern.

The relevant icon is on the right-hand side of the fourth row. Click here first and then choose the pattern and the type of outline you require. After this move the crosshair to one of the vertices you want for your shape. Click the mouse. Moving the crosshair after this will begin the potential outline of your shape. It will be shown as a thin line until you click once more to select the second vertex. Then the line will be fixed in position. It will have the thickness that you selected. Move in turn to all the vertices and click each time to add the new side to the shape. When you have reached the final vertex, click to fix the position. This last side will then be added, linking the current vertex to the first. Double click the mouse and the planned polygon is automatically filled with the chosen pattern.

The fill routine is powerful and able to cope with re-entrant shapes, like a star. It is even possible to cross over sides already added to your polygon to create a pattern of lines forming a series of separate polygons, linked only at certain vertices. Double clicking will still result in the interior areas being filled.

Greater accuracy is possible if you keep <SHIFT> depressed while the vertices are fixed for your shape, although this may limit your artistic creativity. All sides will then be adjusted so that they are either horizontal, vertical or forming 45° diagonals. This can be quite good fun, because the line trailed by the crosshair reveals a degree of intelligence. It will not follow the crosshair to any arbitrary screen position. Instead it stops and seems to think for a little if you depart from the obvious horizontal, vertical or diagonal direction. It then jumps to the nearest point on the paint window which satisfies the angular criterion. If you select a final vertex needing a closing side which is not horizontal, vertical or diagonal, you can still complete the polygon by double clicking. Finishing the shape takes priority over adhering to the correct angle.

Accuracy with the grid

Similar to the angular restriction above is the **Grid On** option which can be selected from the tools menu. Take the pointer to **Tools** on the menu bar. This menu is then superimposed on the paint window:

```
        Undo              (Esc)
     * * * * * * * * * * * * * * * * *
        Grid On
        Transparent On
     * * * * * * * * * * * * * * * * *
        Brush shape
        View Picture
        Size Picture
```

Clicking on **Grid On** will remove the menu and alter the way in which the line indicating the potential side follows the crosshair. Again it does not adopt every position that the crosshair passes through, but instead jumps periodically to the next grid position closest to the current location of the crosshair.

This autonomy of behaviour is particularly apparent when the crosshair is moved vertically. Sometimes the line lags behind the crosshair. Then it will jump ahead.

The restriction of possible vertex positions to predetermined grid locations enforces a degree of precision on to any shape drawn. After completing a shape, the grid can be switched off again. This time the tools menu will be:

```
        Undo              (Esc)
     * * * * * * * * * * * * * * * * *
        Grid Off
        Transparent On
     * * * * * * * * * * * * * * * * *
        Brush shape
        View Picture
        Size Picture
```

Clicking on **Grid Off** returns you to the less controlled drawing style as before.

Circular and oval shapes

The middle icon on the bottom row of the tools palette selects the circle or oval shape. As before, after clicking on this icon you will need to choose the type of outline and shading you want. Then the position, size and shape of the oval or circle is determined using the mouse. Move the crosshair to the position where you want the shape to be, press the button and drag the mouse to form the shape and size you require. At first it is one of the more difficult tools to use, but very satisfying after a little practice. It is ideal for pictures of the Solar System, or complicated molecules! (The orbit of a planet for the former can be obtained by filling the circle with background colour and then using a contrasting fill pattern for the planet and the Sun.)

Constructing an arc

GEM Paint makes it possible to construct arcs of a circle. Strictly speaking, the shape produced will only be a true arc if you fill with the background pattern to erase the area enclosed between the arc and its centre of curvature. This is automatically filled with the current pattern and so will produce sectors of a circle. Another point to note is that you always obtain an angle of 90° subtended by the arc. Smaller arcs will require some erasing as well.

The icon needed is on the left-hand side of the bottom row of the tools palette. Click here, then choose the line width and colour and the pattern you want. After this be very careful in the direction that you move the crosshair after the click which fixes the first end of the arc. This is because the direction of motion will decide on which side of the arc its centre of curvature will lie. It really requires a little practice to obtain the results you expect.

Producing an irregular shape

The bottom right-hand icon will let you build up an irregular or 'free form shape'. Click on this icon and then select the line and fill parameters. Dragging the crosshair around the paint window will then let you build up any shape you like. It fills as soon as you release the button. It you do not close the shape yourself, GEM Paint will link the last point reached to the first.

Keeping the shift key depressed as you drag the crosshair will restrict the outline of your free form shape to lines orientated as horizontals, verticals or 45ı diagonals.

Adding text to a picture

You can add text to your picture by clicking on the right-hand icon of the top row of the tools palette. Make sure that you have chosen the appropriate colour, which will be light if you are adding text to a dark background and vice versa. Then move the pointer to **Typeface** and **Typestyle** in turn on the menu bar, selecting your choice from each menu which appears.

Move back to the paint window and click in the position where you wish your script to begin. A vertical line cursor will indicate where the typed text will start. After you have typed in your first line of text from the keyboard, pressing <ENTER> will move the cursor to a new position, one line further down on the screen. You can continue in this way until you move and reclick the mouse on a new part of the picture. Text can then be entered there. When you have added all the text needed, abandon this mode of GEM Paint's operation by selecting a different icon from the tools palette.

Using the microscope

One of the more attractive words introduced into English by the computer revolution is 'pixel'. Supposedly a near acronym for 'picture element', it generates a truly charming mental image of some interior being lurking inside the computer, a magical cross of pixie and elf and perhaps even related to the 'sprite' so often flaunted in computer animation. The GEM Paint's microscope gives an insight into this unexpected world, more Arthur Rackham than electronics!

Any display generated by a computer is constructed from the pixels present on the screen. They form a matrix of very small rectangles tessellating over the entire screen area. Each is capable of being lit when selected, in various levels of brilliance and, for a colour image, in colours as well. A great deal of memory is required for organising such a screen display.

Before using the GEM microscope, you will need to produce at least part of a picture to be examined in more detail. Then click on the microscope icon. This is on the left-hand side of the top row. After this you can move the pointer to the part of your picture to be examined, and click again. The pointer, will be replaced by the pencil cursor during this routine in GEM Paint. The section of the picture you have chosen will be shown in considerable magnification in the main paint window. Each pixel can be seen in detail. At the same time the same section is shown at its normal size in a small rectangle at the top left of the screen. The position of the magnified section relative to the whole picture is indicated schematically by a second rectangle immediately beneath the first.

Using the pencil and an appropriate colour selected from the palette beneath the two rectangles, the magnified portion can be altered. Fresh pixels can be added or existing ones removed. The small rectangle will be simultaneously updated. When the section is satisfactory, you can return to the original picture by clicking on this rectangle.

Moving outside the paint window

Working with the microscope makes it more important than ever to be able to scroll the paint window vertically and horizontally. This allows parts of the painting which lie outside of the immediate window to be seen. Clicking the mouse on the vertical scroll bar, on the right-hand side of the paint window, and then dragging will adjust the vertical position of the window. The horizontal position can be similarly altered. An alternative to dragging the scroll bars is to click on one of the four arrow boxes at the ends of the scroll bars.

Generating your own pattern

You are not restricted solely to the patterns available on the paint palette but you can also develop some of your own either by modifying, or by totally redesigning, one or more of the existing patterns. It is very probable that at least one of the existing choice will not be appropriate for your current picture.

Decide which pattern that you want to alter or replace. Move the pointer to it and click on this pattern. Then take the pointer to Patterns on the menu bar. This menu will appear:

```
Hide Patterns

********************

Make Pattern
Edit Pattern...

******************

Load Patterns...
Save Patterns...
```

Click on **Edit Pattern.** A dialogue box will now appear on the screen. On the right-hand side there will be a magnified version of part of the pattern while at the top left will be a sample of the repeated pattern at normal size. The bottom left shows the colour choice plus the familiar **OK** and **Cancel** boxes.

If you simply want to alter the existing pattern, select a colour and edit the magnified sample by moving the pointer and clicking the button to add squares of your selected colour. As you do this the overall effect on the repeated pattern will also be shown.

If you want to design an entirely new pattern, move the pointer to the left-hand panel and click the button. The existing pattern will be erased, and you have a clean sheet on which you can start afresh.

When you have completed your design, click on the **OK** box. The new pattern will now appear on the paint palette just as if it had belonged there the whole time.

Saving a picture

When you want to end a session of GEM Paint, you should take the pointer to **Files** on the menu bar:

```
New
Open

***************

Close
Save
Save As...
Abandon

***************

To Output...
Quit
```

Click on **Save As...** and the ITEM SELECTOR will be presented on the screen. The directory will state 'A:\IMAGES*.IMG'. The name you type in for your picture will appear beside **Selection.** After typing the name, perhaps 'TODDY', pressing **<ENTER>** or clicking on **OK** will save the picture. The original display is then restored, but now has the name you chose replacing the asterisk in its title:

A:\IMAGES\TODDY.IMG.

This picture is now stored on the disk. If you select **Quit** on the Files menu to return to GEMAPPS, then click on the 'close' box to reach the root directory and finally double click on the IMAGES icon, you will see it displayed as a folder.

6

The Sinclair Organiser

When you purchase a computer, you may be left with a further decision which must be taken fairly quickly if you are to make the best use of the machine. If the computer that you have bought does not have a selection of appropriate packages bundled with it you will need to discover which is the best software to operate it. Here the Sinclair PC has a definite advantage over some of its rivals because it comes complete with the Organiser software.

Advantages of the Organiser software

The Sinclair Organiser provides a simple word processor, a database, and several other useful features, like its calculator. For many people these facilities will be sufficient to meet their personal administrative needs for a long time, making it unnecessary to purchase any other similar software. However it might be felt advisable to look at some of the other domestic or business packages which feature similar, although extended, applications to the Sinclair Organiser.

Even here the Organiser is helpful because it gives you an excellent example of the types of activity where the use of a computer is particularly beneficial. It shows you how a good quality word processor contributes to both your professional work and also purely personal correspondence and notes. The data handling facility is a gentle introduction to the world of database management. Similarly its arithmetical aspects will permit just a little insight into the world of spreadsheets.

Although the Organiser cannot fairly be expected to compete with a dedicated integrated package, nevertheless it does educate you and familiarise you with the potentiality of this type of software. When you reach the stage of needing to expand the capability of your system, with the experience of the Organiser behind you, you should be able to select the right software with confidence.

Starting the Sinclair Organiser

Before you begin your first session with the organiser software make sure that you have prepared a back-up copy of the organiser disk which was provided with your

Sinclair PC. This is essential in case something goes wrong and the disk you are using becomes corrupted. If you accidentally spoil your initial disk by failing to work with a back-up you will still probably get help from your local dealer, but it is a bad habit to acquire.

Switch on the computer and boot it with your back-up MS-DOS disk, setting the correct time and date. How to do this is explained clearly in the manual provided with the Sinclair PC and again at the beginning of the MS-DOS section of this book, in chapter 10. Remove the MS-DOS disk and replace it with the back-up copy of the Organiser disk which you have prepared.

Now, at the MS-DOS A-prompt, type **ORG**, or **org** in lower case, and press the <ENTER> key:

    A>ORG

You will see the screen prompt:

    Sinclair Organiser now loading... Please Wait

After a moderate delay, the initial Organiser display appears, naming the options you have available in the software, together with the usual copyright message:

SINCLAIR ORGANISER   Safe   Saturday 07-Jan-89 8:16am

               SINCLAIR ORGANISER Main Menu

                      Recall by Index
                         Diary
                      Word Processor
                   New Address & Cardfile
                      Search for data
                        Calculator
                        Templates
                  Exit SINCLAIR ORGANISER

RunALC v1.17. Copyright (c) Clasma S/W Ltd 1985-8.
                                       All Rights reserved

This display remains for thirty seconds. Then the software decides that you have had long enough to decide the choice you should make from the menu. It concludes you do not know what to do. It therefore prompts you further with the added message:

 Help
Menu of options available
Choose from options using Up-Down then press Enter
You may also press the Highlighted letter of the choice required

This way of selecting from a menu is quite common in the software you may eventually acquire for your Sinclair PC. It is employed, for example, in some versions of the word processor WordStar. Experiment with it now. Pressing the cursor-up key will make the highlighting bar on the menu ripple upwards, starting again each time from the bottom of the menu. The opposite effect is achieved with the cursor-down key. When the highlighting bar has arrived at a suitable destination, you press <ENTER>. A quicker alternative is simply to press the initial letter of the choice you want. The tidily minded may find this redundancy a little unnecessary.

The first option we will discuss is the Organiser's diary. First, however, a brief note is needed about a possible problem which you may already have encountered.

Getting the time right

You may have loaded the Organiser software without first setting the current date and time while the MS-DOS disk was still in the disk drive. This omission will be noticed immediately by the Organiser. It needs to know exactly where in time it is so that it can start organising you. It does not believe the MS-DOS default date of 1st Jan, 1980.

This is similar to the very early episode of Dr. Who in which he unwittingly jammed the controls in reverse and began hurtling back to inevitable destruction in the Big Bang. A fail-safe on his Tardis anxiously drew his attention to the problem with a series of increasingly desperate prompts including prehistoric footage of rampaging dinosaurs.

Sadly the Organiser software is not quite so ambitious. Nevertheless it does make its point reasonably forcefully with a screen message highlighted on a red background:

```
SINCLAIR ORGANISER      Safe     Tuesday 01-Jan-80 12:32am

                        Problem!
             System date before date of last use
                        01-Aug-88

                  Exit to system (MS-DOS)
                        Continue
```

You can return to MS-DOS by pressing E. Then tell the Sinclair what the date and time are by using the **MS-DOS DATE** and **TIME** commands, as explained in the Sinclair PC manual or here in chapter 10. You do not need to reinsert the MS-DOS disk in order to do this. After the correction type **ORG** followed by <ENTER> to resume the Organiser software as above.

Alternatively, when you see the warning prompt you can press C on the keyboard. The word 'Continue' will flash for a while and then the initial Organiser display is shown without alteration to the date and time.

The Organiser diary

The Organiser's diary is an impressive part of the software. After using it for a little while you really do start to think in terms of a magic electronic book, whose pages are always there, ready to be turned over to display messages entered on previous occasions. It is really a pity you cannot fit the Sinclair PC conveniently into your jacket pocket or bag, because the diary would be extremely convenient to have nearby the whole day. Fortunately so much of the individual's personal organisation is done working at a particular location in the home that this will not be too much of a disadvantage. Of course, the real solution would be to have a Sinclair PC at home and another at work... Then you would only need to carry your, continually updated, Organiser floppy disk round with you. As it is a secure three and a half inch disk in a heavy duty plastic case, this would not be a problem.

Opening the diary

You enter the diary application from the Organiser's main menu by highlighting the appropriate choice with the cursor keys and pressing <ENTER>, or just by pressing **D**. Whichever method you select, the main menu is erased except for the diary option. This flashes and then the display alters to show the last month that was consulted in the diary, like this:

```
                      January 1989
---------------------------------------------------------
  Mon      Tue      Wed      Thu      Fri      Sat      Sun
---------------------------------------------------------
                                                        1
---------------------------------------------------------
   2        3        4        5        6        7        8
---------------------------------------------------------
   9       10       11       12       13       14       15
---------------------------------------------------------
  16       17       18       19       20       21       22
---------------------------------------------------------
  23       24       25       26       27       28       29
---------------------------------------------------------
  30       31
---------------------------------------------------------
```

The current date is still shown at the top right-hand corner of the display. This diary format is neat and easy to read. Short entries can be made for each day, or a longer entry for the month placed at the top of the calendar sheet. The box for each day can contain six characters. The monthly message can be two lines long with up to 59 and 58 characters each, respectively.

When you arrive at the diary, the Sinclair Organiser again allows you thirty seconds to gather your thoughts. After that a prompt appears beneath the calendar to let you decide what should happen next. (A rather glaring grammatical error here fails to agree the subject and verb!)

```
Calendar for January. Type short notes onto calendar.
Arrows moves, PgDn-PgUp-Next/Prev month Esc-Exit F9-Show notes
on highlighted date ^F4-Find notes Del-Delete short note
```

Moving around the diary

One day of the month displayed is highlighted by a colour reversal. The rest of the calendar is depicted in blue on white, but the current day is shown with white foreground and blue background.

You move around the calendar using the cursor keys. Cursor left takes you back to the day before. Cursor right moves the highlighting to the next day. Cursor up goes back to the same day of the previous week. Cursor down advances the day highlighted by one week.

Moving to the next month is achieved using <PgDn> on the key pad. The same day of the month is selected as before. So if the diary is currently highlighting January 7th 1989, pressing <PgDn> will take you to February 7th 1989. In a similar way, <PgUp> goes back to December 7th 1988.

It is important that you type lightly, without holding any keys down excessively. Otherwise you will probably overshoot the date that you are trying to find. Also when using <PgUp> and <PgDn> you must make sure that <Num Lock> is off. If it is not, you will simply enter numbers at the current date highlighted.

Entering a short daily note

A brief, six character message can be entered for any day. You only need to find the correct place on the month's calendar and then type it in from the keyboard. The background blue for the day is immediately replaced by white and the letters you are typing are highlighted. When you press <ENTER> the note is displayed in white on blue until you move to another day. It then reverts to the blue on white used throughout the diary.

If you attempt to type a longer note than is allowed, your Sinclair PC will beep. If you wish to alter a note, an easy way is to press <ENTER> and then <Del>. The note is then removed and you can either retype or ignore that date completely.

Adding a longer day note

A diary which allowed you to make entries only six letters long would not be very useful. Fortunately you can make a longer note for a particular day with the Sinclair Organiser. Suppose that, although the assumed 'current date' in the diary is January

7th 1989, you wish to go ahead to February 14th and place a message to yourself there. Use <PgDn> to go from January to February and then find the 14th with the cursor keys. You could, of course, just use the cursor keys without pressing <PgDn> first, but this would take longer.

When you reach February 14th, press the grey <F10> key at the top of the keyboard. This new menu will now be superimposed on the calendar:

```
                 Diary Menu : February

                      New Entry
              Show entries for 14-Feb-89
                     Find Entries
              Go to today : 07-Jan-89
              Month detail : February
```

If you do not choose any of the selection offered, the usual prompting occurs with the added display beneath the calendar as before:

```
Help
Menu of options available.
Choose from options using Up-Down then press Enter
You may also press the Highlighted letter of the choice required
```

What you intend to do is enter information for the day, so either press **N**, or make sure that 'New Entry' is highlighted before pressing <ENTER>. The menu, and the help prompt if present, are both removed and this box appears on the calendar:

```
                 Diary Day Note


     Date       14-Feb-89
     From       12:00am
     To         12:00am
     Note
     Type       Note     Alarm    Past    To Do    Done
```

Again if you do nothing at all after the usual delay more advice will be displayed at the bottom of the screen:

```
Day Note on 14-Feb-89 Enter/Edit day note into Diary.
Use arrows & editing keys. Esc-to accept ^F0-Exit without
entering day note
From & To times are optional. Alarm will set this note as an
alarm
```

At the moment you can just concentrate on adding a single note for the day. Press <ENTER> twice, or use the cursor keys, to reach the line marked 'Note'. Then add your message to yourself for this future date:

Date	14-Feb-89				
From	12:00am				
To	12:00am				
Note	Deliver card to Pauline				
Type	Note	Alarm	Past	To Do	Done

Your note can be up to 40 characters long. Now press <Esc>. The box will disappear, returning the display to the calendar. You will now see that the date has been highlighted. This is to remind you, when you look through the diary later, that there is something significant to check, on this particular day.

Looking through your diary

When you want to search through your diary to examine the various messages you have inserted, first you load the Organiser software and select the diary from the main menu. Then use <PgDn> and <PgUp> to go to different months in turn. You will see the brief notes that you have placed on the calendar, together with highlighted dates indicating where a longer entry has been jotted down.

To investigate what has been entered into the diary for a highlighted date, simply use the cursor keys to move the blue rectangle to that day. Then press <ENTER>. For example, assuming that you have placed the message given in the last section into the Organiser's diary, pressing <ENTER> on February 14th will show this:

```
14-Feb-89          Day
14-Feb-89                    Deliver card to Pauline
```

The message is displayed in a new window which appears at the bottom of the screen beneath the calendar.

If you now press <Esc> this window will be removed. However, you can retain it, use the cursor keys to move from day to day, and any relevant messages for the selected date will be displayed. If there is no message, not only is the window left showing nothing but the date but, in addition at the top left-hand side of the display, the words 'SINCLAIR ORGANISER' are replaced by a flashing prompt: 'Nothing found'. White text on red background is used - the Organiser's colour scheme for anything it feels should make you pay extra attention.

Another way of discovering what has been recorded for a particular day, is to go to that date and then press <F10>. Again, the diary menu will be shown:

Diary Menu : February

New Entry
Show entries for 14-Feb-89
Find Entries
Go to today : 07-Jan-89
Month detail : February

This time select the second option, by using cursor keys and <ENTER> or simply pressing **S**. The message will be shown at the bottom of the screen.

```
14-Feb-89          Day
14-Feb-89                        Deliver card to Pauline
```

A third technique for examining the diary content for a specific date is using <F9>. Pressing this when the relevant day is highlighted on the calendar will show any notes. Use <Esc> to return to the calendar as before.

Adding additional day notes

You are not restricted to a single note for each day. More can be added by going to the day required and pressing <F10> to summon the diary menu. This time press **N** for a new entry. The same window will appear as earlier. Any existing message is not shown on this window. As before, ignore the From and To options and type the extra note on the fourth line. Press <Esc> to enter it:

```
               Diary Day Note
Date      14-Feb-89
From      12:00am
To        12:00am
Note      Send flowers to Michelle.
Type        Note      Alarm    Past    To Do    Done
```

After you have typed in your extra note and pressed <Esc> the display returns once more to the unadorned calendar format. Since the relevant date is still highlighted, you can view your extra details just by pressing <ENTER>:

```
14-Feb-89          Day
14-Feb-89                        Deliver card to Pauline
                                 Send flowers to Michelle
```

Specifying a time

The Organiser lets you attach times to the notes you enter for each day. If you press <F10> while 14th Feb is still highlighted, and then select the new entry option again by pressing **N**, you could add the note shown below:

```
               Diary Day Note
Date      14-Feb-89
From      05:15pm
To        06:15pm
Note      Take present to Lucy.
Type        Note      Alarm    Past    To Do    Done
```

NOTE: When the times are entered you must keep to the two digit format for both hours and minutes. Failing to do this will lead to an annoyed beep from the Sinclair PC's speaker.

Press <Esc> to enter the message. Now repeat the process to enter a visit to the bank and finally a reminder about doing some work for the day:

<pre>
                    Diary Day Note

    Date   14-Feb-89
    From   12:30pm
    To   01:00pm
    Note   Visit Nat West and cash cheque
    Type   Note   Alarm   Past   To Do   Done
</pre>

<pre>
                    Diary Day Note

    Date   14-Feb-89
    From   07:30pm
    To   11:59pm
    Note   Put 'do not disturb' on study door!
    Type   Note   Alarm   Past   To Do   Done
</pre>

Now looking at your notes for the day will show that the Sinclair Organiser has sorted the timed notes into their correct order, rather than the one in which they were entered. The untimed notes are placed at the end of the list and in the order you used:

<pre>
14-Feb-89   Day
14-Feb-89 12:30pm-01:00pm Visit Nat West and cash cheque
          05:15pm-06:15pm Take present to Lucy
          07:30pm-11:59pm Put 'do not disturb' outside study
                           Deliver card to Pauline
                           Send flowers to Michelle
</pre>

You can begin to see why the software has been called 'Organiser'!

An automatic reminder

You can set up a diary entry with an automatic alarm. First go to the date concerned, press <F10> to obtain the diary menu and then **N** for new entry. Enter the relevant times for 'From' and 'To'. An alarm requires these to be set. Type in the note and finally highlight 'Alarm' on the last line of the day note. This is done with the cursor-right key:

<pre>
                    Diary Day Note

    Date   21-Feb-89
    From   03:30pm
    To   04:30pm
    Note   Take Rufus to the vet.
    Type   Note   Alarm   Past   To Do   Done
</pre>

Finally press <Esc> to enter the note. The day will be highlighted on the calendar. Whenever you check the notes for this particular day, you will realise that the alarm

Figure 6.1: An automatic diary

has been set for this note by the presence of an additional 'A' in front of the message.

You can check whether the alarm works by pretending that you have actually reached February 21st in 'real time'. First you must leave the Organiser software and return to MS-DOS in order to reset the time and date.

Leaving the Organiser

You can exit an Organiser application by pressing <**Esc**>. The main menu will then be shown again:

```
SINCLAIR ORGANISER Main Menu

        Recall by Index
             Diary
        Word Processor
    New Address & Cardfile
        Search for data
          Calculator
           Templates
    Exit SINCLAIR ORGANISER
```

The last choice on this menu is the one you require. Select this with the cursor keys and press <ENTER>, or press **E**. You will now see the Organiser request confirmation of your choice:

```
Exit to System (MS-DOS)

         Yes
         No
```

Press **Y** and you will return to the MS-DOS A-prompt.

Testing the alarm

You should now use the MS-DOS commands, DATE and TIME, to set the supposedly current date to 21st February 1989 and the time to 3.25pm. (Check the relevant section of chapter 10 if you are unsure of these commands.) The choice of time allows you to test the alarm that has been set in the diary, provided that you load the Organiser again quickly enough!

Now, to continue with the subterfuge, go to 21st Feb in the calendar. Watch the time at the top right-hand corner of the screen approaching the alarm time of 3.30pm. It is quite exciting. When you have caught up with the time specified for the note a red band appears at the top of the screen with the white, flashing message:

```
21-Feb-89 03:30pm Take Rufus to the vet.
```

This is combined with a discordant trill which repeats indefinitely until you press <ENTER>. Once the alarm has been sounded it is deactivated and will not repeat, even if you cheat on setting the date again.

Searching for an item

Looking through a conventional diary, trying to find a particular entry or reference, can be extremely time consuming and easy to get wrong. You only need accidentally to turn two pages at once for a vital day to be missed. The Organiser proves especially useful in such circumstances, because it can be set up to look for a key word or phrase throughout the diary.

Suppose you are trying to list all the birthdays during the year which you have jotted down at different times. First go to January, then obtain the diary menu with <F10> and press **F** for 'Find Entries'. This window will appear:

```
              Diary Notes Find

Find what?
Exclude what?
Range?             Day   Week   2 Weeks   Month   Year All
```

For a easy search, just type in the item required, ignoring the 'exclude' option. Similarly highlight 'year' in the range:

```
                      Diary Notes Find
Find what? birthday
Exclude what?
Range?                 Day    Week    2 Weeks   Month   Year   All
```

Begin the search by pressing <Esc>. You will now see displayed at the bottom of the screen a list of all the daily notes with 'birthday' included:

```
            Year           birthday
27-Feb-89                  Rita's birthday. Get present.
27-Jul-89                  Lucy's birthday. Get card with frog.
13-Aug-89                  Mike's birthday. Get present.
25-Sep-89                  Tessa's birthday. Get present.
18-Nov-89                  My birthday. Bottle of Jack Daniels!!!
```

The use of 'exclude' can be seen in this further example:

```
                      Diary Notes Find
Find what? birthday
Exclude what?          present
Range?                 Day    Week    2 Weeks   Month   Year   All
```

Pressing <Esc> now leads to a simpler list:

```
            Year           birthday
27-Jul-89                  Lucy's birthday. Get card with frog.
18-Nov-89                  My birthday. Bottle of Jack Daniels!!!
```

After all, everybody knows that installing a computer is meant to lead to an overall reduction in expenditure...

Altering a note

The Organiser also allows you to overwrite a note in the diary. To do this go to the day concerned and show the notes by pressing <ENTER>. Highlight the note you wish to change by using the cursor keys. Then press <F10>. A slightly different menu will appear:

```
                Diary Menu : 05-Jul-89

                      New Entry
                Change Highlighted note
                      Find notes
                Go to today : 05-Jan-89

                   Exit to Main Menu
```

Pressing C will now let you alter the note chosen.

Deleting a note

You will also want to alter diary entries from time to time. Perhaps, after reflection, you decide that your original schedule for February 14th is too crowded. Use the combination of <PgDn>, <PgUp> and the cursor keys to highlight the date. Press <ENTER> and the notes for the day will be shown. Now you can highlight the different notes in turn with the cursor-up and cursor-down keys. Note that you have to use both. The highlighting bar will not automatically reappear at the top if you keep pressing cursor-down key, nor at the bottom if you keep pressing the cursor-up key. This is a little unusual with this type of software. Instead the flashing 'Nothing found' will be displayed at the top of the screen.

Considering the various possibilities, your attention is focused on the third note for the day:

```
14-Feb-89        Day
14-Feb-89 12:30pm-01:00pm Visit Nat West and cash cheque
          05:15pm-06:15pm Take present to Lucy
          07:30pm-11:59pm Put 'do not disturb' outside study
                          Deliver card to Pauline
                          Send flowers to Michelle
```

With this choice highlighted, press the <Del> key. You now see an additional message with white text on red background:

```
                 Delete Note ?

                 Yes
                 No
```

Either choice can be highlighted with cursor-up or cursor-down, both keys toggling between the two possibilities. Press <ENTER> when 'Yes' is chosen or just the Y key. In standard Organiser fashion, the Yes choice flashes and then the new set of notes is displayed:

```
14-Feb-89        Day
14-Feb-89 12:30pm-01:00pm Visit Nat West and cash cheque
          05:15pm-06:15pm Take present to Lucy
                          Deliver card to Pauline
                          Send flowers to Michelle
```

Adding a detail for the month

At the top of the calendar are two lines on which a message may be placed relating to the whole month, here chosen as April with <PgDn>. The detail facility is accessed via the main menu by pressing <F10> and then M:

```
                Diary Menu : April

                    New Entry
            Show entries for 14-Apr-89
                  Find Entries
            Go to today : 07-Jan-89
            Month detail : April
```

No window appears beneath the calendar. Instead the cursor indicating the start of your note begins flashing immediately beneath the name of the month, allowing you to type in your relevant comment:

```
                    April 1989
April is the coolest month and
Breeding pandas takes a lot of patience
-----------------------------------------------------------
  Mon     Tue     Wed     Thu     Fri     Sat     Sun
-----------------------------------------------------------
                                                    1
-----------------------------------------------------------
   3       4       5       6       7       8       9
-----------------------------------------------------------
  10      11      12      13      14      15      16
-----------------------------------------------------------
  17      18      19      20      21      22      23
-----------------------------------------------------------
  24      25      26      27      28      29      30
-----------------------------------------------------------
-----------------------------------------------------------
```

The first line of the note can hold 59 characters and the second 58. <ENTER> toggles between the two lines until the month detail is confirmed by <Esc>.

Updating the disk

When using a twin disk-drive personal computer combined with some specific piece of software, perhaps the WordStar word processor on an Amstrad 1512, you become quite used to the way your software is held on one of the disks while the data used by the software, the content of your documents, is stored on the other. At intervals during your work, each disk may be accessed in turn. This is not an inconvenience.

The Sinclair Organiser operates in a similar way, except that there is only one drive involved and so the Organiser software and the data it is handling have to reside on the same disk. This inevitably leads to slight hiccough as the system attends to its internal housekeeping. A warning will be given at the top of the display:

```
                    Not Safe
```

The disk drive will not necessarily be accessed during the whole of the time this prompt appears, but its presence indicates that the disk is not fully updated. Another warning which is given when the disk is being accessed is:

```
Disk, wait...
```

The default message displayed most of the time is 'Safe'. This means that the disk is currently up to date.

Security of your diary

If you come to rely upon your Organiser as a personal diary, you will have to consider the potential problem of a corrupted disk leading to loss of important information, vital dates and appointments. The solution for this is to make regular back-up copies of your Organiser disk at frequent intervals. The MS-DOS diskcopy command can be used to do this, as detailed in the Sinclair PC manual, or chapter 9 below. How often you perform this process will be a matter of personal faith in your Sinclair PC. A good rule, though, is that often is preferable to seldom.

7

An organiser database

The Sinclair Organiser's introduction to the various types of software application available to the personal computer user is continued in its database option. Although limited in comparison with the data handling software you are able to purchase, it does provide a useful overview of the facilities found in a typical database.

General structure of a database

You can form a clear mental picture of a database by thinking of an office filing cabinet. The different drawers, each containing folders further organised into separate sections with titled divider cards, suggests the type of logical and systematic store which you can create. The cabinet is under the jurisdiction of a very efficient secretary who can search for, and find, specific items, even when given only a minimal guide to where the information might be. Now imagine that all of this is handled just by the program and data held on a floppy disk placed into the Sinclair PC and you can appreciate the power of storage and recall achieved through the computer.

The fundamental entity in a database is the 'record'. This is a collection of information on a specific subject, perhaps everything relating to a particular employee in a firm. The set of all such records is referred to as a 'file'. The categories into which a specific record is divided are called 'fields'. To continue the example, obvious fields present in the record will be name, age, salary, years of service...

An essential operation in a database is the search for a particular record, given only part of the information present, though sufficient to identify it. Typically the surname of an employee will single out the record required, though other information could be used in many cases. The part of the record used in such a search, here the surname, is called the 'key field'. These terms can all be illustrated via the Sinclair Organiser's data handling operations.

Creating a database with the Sinclair Organiser

When you intend starting a database with the Organiser, you begin at the main menu.

Highlight the fourth option and press <**ENTER**> or alternatively just press **N**:

```
SINCLAIR ORGANISER Main Menu

        Recall by Index
             Diary
         Word Processor
   New Address & Cardfile
        Search for data
          Calculator
           Templates
    Exit SINCLAIR ORGANISER
```

This will give you 'New Address & Cardfile', introduced with a further menu:

```
          New data in...

         Address card
      General Cardfile

       Exit to Main Menu
```

There is only really one significant choice here because the address card option has such a highly specific fixed format. This is displayed if you select **Address card** or press **A**:

```
Address Index
Index under...Category

Company                         Date
Contact
Posi'n     Cross
Dept.      Reference
Street     to...
City
Zip  Phone 1
CountryPhone 2
Dear...Twx/Email
Details
```

The inclusion of room for the Zip code reveals the origin of the Organiser software even more obviously than the occasional spelling of the name as 'Organizer'.

Selecting the General Cardfile

This selection can be used for a variety of applications and is the Sinclair Organiser's equivalent of the record in a database. To obtain it press **G**, or highlight General Cardfile and press <**ENTER**>. A window is then shown at the bottom right hand corner of the screen, clearly designed to resemble the sort of physical, cardboard card that you might find in a typical office filing tray. Its overall format is like this:

```
**Cardfile*Index**************************
* Index                    Date 23-Feb-89*
*_____ *
*                                        *
*                                        *
*                                        *
*                                        *
*                                        *
*                                        *
*                                        *
*                                        *
*                                        *
*                                        *
******************************************
```

The main area of the card is 40 characters wide and contains 10 separate rows. Obviously there is potential here for a great deal of information, but you must remember the limitation imposed by the amount of data which can be stored on the Sinclair PC's floppy disk. It is perhaps better to regard the size of the card as permitting a clear layout for the items you enter rather than an invitation to be very explicit about every possible detail.

As you fill in the card, the cursor position jumps to the next relevant location each time <ENTER> is pressed. Initially the card is requesting an index for the record. Suppose you type in 'CAT'. This is automatically placed at the top of the card:

```
**Cardfile*Index**************************
* Index CAT                Date 23-Feb-89*
*_____ *
*                                        *
*                                        *
*                                        *
*                                        *
*                                        *
*                                        *
*                                        *
*                                        *
*                                        *
*                                        *
******************************************
```

You press <ENTER> to show that this first piece of information is complete. The top line of the card now alters to prompt you about the next item to be typed:

```
**Cardfile*CardDate**********************
* Index                    Date 23-Feb-89*
*_____ *
*                                         *
*                                         *
*                                         *
*                                         *
*                                         *
*                                         *
*                                         *
*                                         *
*                                         *
*                                         *
******************************************
```

You can now type any date you wish. Just pressing <ENTER> will assume the one already present. Again the text at the top of the card changes to show how to fill in the card. You can now begin to complete the main section of the card:

```
**Cardfile*CardText**********************
* Index CAT                Date 23-Feb-89*
*_____ *
* NAME Toddy                              *
* COLOUR Ginger                           *
* AGE One year                            *
* HOBBY Climbing trouser legs             *
* DISPOSITION Wistful and patient         *
*                                         *
*                                         *
*                                         *
*                                         *
*                                         *
******************************************
```

When you have finished, <Esc> completes the process. To create another card you again select 'New Address & Cardfile' and then press G.

Creating fields in your cardfile

Following the above procedure, you could establish a limited database, on PreRaphaelite artists perhaps, allowing one card, or record, per artist. The surname of the artist will serve as the entry for 'Index' at the top of the card. Regard this as the key field. The date option here will be allowed to default to the date current on the Organiser, although it could be used as, perhaps, the date of birth of the artist if that information is available. When the main part of the card is reached, the 'CardText', the information is structured into four fields. These are the Christian names of the artist, the years of birth and death and, just one, specimen work of art:

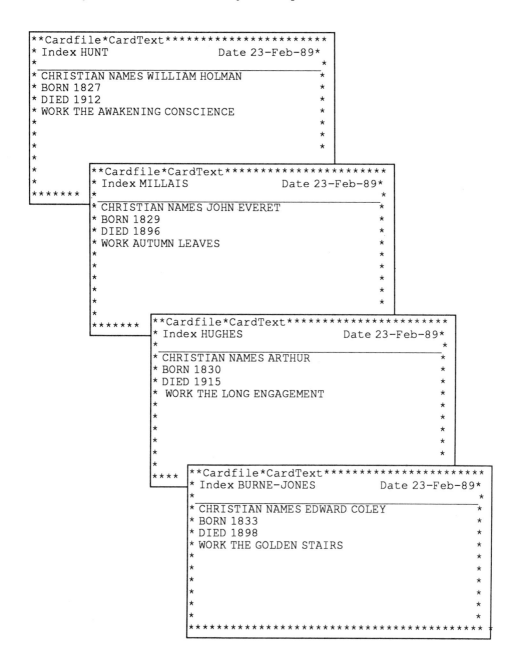

```
**Cardfile*CardText***********************
* Index HUNT                Date 23-Feb-89*
*                                          *
*‾CHRISTIAN NAMES WILLIAM HOLMAN          *
* BORN 1827                               *
* DIED 1912                               *
* WORK THE AWAKENING CONSCIENCE           *
*                                         *
*                                         *
*                                         *
*
*           **Cardfile*CardText***********************
*           * Index MILLAIS            Date 23-Feb-89*
*******     *                                        *
            *‾CHRISTIAN NAMES JOHN EVERET           *
            * BORN 1829                             *
            * DIED 1896                             *
            * WORK AUTUMN LEAVES                    *
            *                                       *
            *                                       *
            *                                       *
            *                                       *
            *                                       *
            *
   *******  **Cardfile*CardText***********************
            * Index HUGHES             Date 23-Feb-89*
            *                                         *
            *‾CHRISTIAN NAMES ARTHUR                 *
            * BORN 1830                              *
            * DIED 1915                              *
            *  WORK THE LONG ENGAGEMENT              *
            *                                        *
            *                                        *
            *                                        *
            *                                        *
            *                                        *
            *
       **** **Cardfile*CardText***********************
            * Index BURNE-JONES        Date 23-Feb-89*
            *                                         *
            *‾CHRISTIAN NAMES EDWARD COLEY           *
            * BORN 1833                              *
            * DIED 1898                              *
            * WORK THE GOLDEN STAIRS                 *
            *                                        *
            *                                        *
            *                                        *
            *                                        *
            *                                        *
            ******************************************
```

Searching a database

A database without a searching facility would not be a great deal of use. You could still store information in it and would naturally be able to look through your records yourself. However, this would necessarily take a long time and be rather like trying to locate something in a large library without the help of a resident librarian.

With automatic searching, the speed of the computer in processing data can be applied in a meaningful way to your information handling. Without it, a database loses its purpose.

Using a key field

One way in which you can look for a particular item is to use the 'Recall by Index' option from the main menu. This involves the first item you entered on to your record and which acts as the key field of the search that takes place.

To use this method you need to return to the main menu and select the first choice, either with cursor and <ENTER> keys or by pressing **R**:

```
SINCLAIR ORGANISER Main Menu

        Recall by Index
             Diary
        Word Processor
    New Address & Cardfile
        Search for data
           Calculator
           Templates
      Exit SINCLAIR ORGANISER
```

You will then see a small blue window appear near the top of the display, requesting the name entered in the key field:

```
Recall what ? :
```

In typical Sinclair Organiser fashion, if you do not make any further entry a help window will be placed at the bottom of the screen after the usual delay:

```
Help
Recall data from database Type what to recall from database &
press Enter.
Esc-Exit. Data will be recalled from all Cardfiles. Type part
of request for vague recalls!
```

Remembering the content of the first record made in this rather small database, type 'HUNT'. The relevant record will now be located by the Organiser and displayed at the bottom right hand corner of the display:

```
**Cardfile*CardText*********************
* Index HUNT                Date 23-Feb-89*
*_____*
* CHRISTIAN NAMES WILLIAM HOLMAN         *
* BORN 1827                              *
* DIED 1912                              *
* WORK THE AWAKENING CONSCIENCE          *
*                                        *
*                                        *
*                                        *
*                                        *
*                                        *
*                                        *
*****************************************
```

Pressing **<Esc>** will take you back to the Organiser's main menu. Any of the records in the database may be checked in this direct fashion, provided that the index is available as a key field.

Equating upper and lower case

Fortunately the Organiser does not expect you to remember correctly whether a particular record's index was originally typed in upper or lower case. This means that if you enter 'Burne-Jones', you will still obtain the record required:

Recall what ? : Burne-Jones

Typing the name in this way does retrieve the appropriate card:

```
**Cardfile*CardText*********************
* Index BURNE-JONES          Date 23-Feb-89*
*_____*
* CHRISTIAN NAMES EDWARD COLEY           *
* BORN 1833                              *
* DIED 1898                              *
* WORK THE GOLDEN STAIRS                 *
*                                        *
*                                        *
*                                        *
*                                        *
*                                        *
*                                        *
*****************************************
```

Data matching

One feature of databases is data matching. This is the ability to retrieve some item of data back from the database when the complete key field identifying it is not known.

It is similar to the process of looking through Yellow Pages for the plumber and saying to yourself 'He said his name was Bert and had a shop near the station'. Armed with this highly specific information, you decide that 'B.H.Forsythe-Smith, Sanitary Engineer, 34b, Railway Cuttings, Leamington Spar' is probably the address to pass on to your solicitor. In the same way any self-respecting database will endeavour to find something in its records which is reasonably close to your inquiry.

The Organiser software does not appear to make any specific reference in its screen prompts to the existence of a this matching facility, but it is only being modest. Although there is no explicit format given for the way in which incomplete data may be entered, the Organiser's 'Near match' option offers this facility.

You can test it with the miniature database that you have set up. Suppose you have a vague recollection of a painter whose name began 'Mill...'. You guess and decide that he might be 'MILLER'. To retrieve information held under this name, press **R** at the main menu:

```
SINCLAIR ORGANISER Main Menu

        Recall by Index
             Diary
         Word Processor
     New Address & Cardfile
        Search for data
          Calculator
           Templates
      Exit SINCLAIR ORGANISER
```

and then type 'MILLER' at the request for an index:

```
        Recall what ? : MILLER
```

After you have pressed **<ENTER>**, the Sinclair Organiser will beep and present you with one of its red and white warnings:

```
             Problem
     Recalled data not found
             MILLER

          Near match
          Re-enter
           Abort
```

If you freeze at this point the Organiser will politely allow you the usual period and then provide the further information:

```
Help
Recall Data Not Found! Data recalled is not in the database.
Near match-for the nearest match to your request.Re-enter-
Goes back to the recall prompt. Abort-Exit to Main Menu.
```

The choice you should select now is 'Near match' and so press **N**. Without any difficulty, the Organiser decides that, amongst its collection of records, the Millais card is the nearest to your requirement. This is what is presented on the screen:

```
**Cardfile*CardText*********************
* Index MILLAIS           Date 23-Feb-89*
*  _____        *
* CHRISTIAN NAMES JOHN EVERETT          *
* BORN 1829                             *
* DIED 1896                             *
* WORK AUTUMN LEAVES                    *
*                                       *
*                                       *
*                                       *
*                                       *
*                                       *
*                                       *
*****************************************
```

Finding several matches

The search illustrated above led to an unambiguous result. Suppose, however, that the Organiser could not decide quite so easily which of its records most closely matched your entry. For example, you might have entered 'HINT' as the keyword expected to retrieve the information on Holman Hunt. The screen dialogue would proceed like this:

```
              Recall what ? : HINT

                   Problem
            Recalled data not found
                    HINT

                 Near match
                  Re-enter
                   Abort
```

Selecting **Near match** will now give a window with more than one match found:

```
              Index name          Card
     HUGHES                     Cardfile
     HUNT                       Cardfile
```

In the help information which is displayed after a pause, another superb American spelling occurs, presumably to fit the word on to the line on which it appears!

```
Help
Recalled list shows Keys & Cardfile that nearest match the
request.
Up-Down-Scroll thru list Esc-Exit Enter-Select highlighted
data F4-Recall prompt
```

You can then examine all the choices given on the list. Pressing **<ENTER>** will display the currently highlighted record:

```
**Cardfile*CardText**********************
* Index HUNT              Date 23-Feb-89*
*_____       *
* CHRISTIAN NAMES WILLIAM HOLMAN          *
* BORN 1827                               *
* DIED 1912                               *
* WORK THE AWAKENING CONSCIENCE           *
*                                         *
*                                         *
*                                         *
*                                         *
*                                         *
*                                         *
******************************************
```

If this is the record you need, press **<Esc>** when you have finished examining it. However if it is not the correct record, press **<F4>**. This will then take you back to your initial request:

                    Recall what ? : HINT

Now **<ENTER>**, followed by **N**, will return you to the list of near matches again and allow you to select another record with the cursor keys:

	Index name	Card
HUGHES		Cardfile
HUNT		Cardfile

In this way you can could look through a series of cards until you find the one you want.

Altering a record

It is quite easy to alter a record held in the Organiser database. Suppose, for example, you have found out more about the artist Arthur Hughes and now want to add the painting 'April Love' to the appropriate record. (This is a melancholy girl in a purple dress under a tree, often used on chocolate boxes.) To alter the relevant record, you go to the main menu just as before, and select **Recall by Index**. Then you give HUGHES as the key field or index and retrieve the correct card:

```
**Cardfile*CardText***********************
* Index HUGHES              Date 23-Feb-89*
*_____*
* CHRISTIAN NAMES ARTHUR                  *
* BORN 1830                               *
* DIED 1915                               *
* WORK THE LONG ENGAGEMENT                *
*                                         *
*                                         *
*                                         *
*                                         *
*                                         *
*******************************************
```

After this, press <F10>. You will see it has a different effect in this context from its role in the Organiser diary, detailed in the previous chapter. Instead it now it displays this choice:

Cardfile Menu :

Find text in Cardfile
Delete

Exit to Main Menu

As you are going to add something to the main part of the record, you need to display the card text. To do this, press **F**. When you are further prompted to specify some item on the main part of the card it does not really matter what you type, provided that it is something already present. You could, say, just enter 'THE':

Find what ? THE

You are then shown the card with the cursor flashing on the name of the current painting. Press <ENTER> to go to the next line. You can now add the second painting's name:

```
**Cardfile*CardText***********************
* Index HUGHES              Date 23-Feb-89*
*_____*
* CHRISTIAN NAMES ARTHUR                  *
* BORN 1830                               *
* DIED 1915                               *
* WORK THE LONG ENGAGEMENT                *
* APRIL LOVE                              *
*                                         *
*                                         *
*                                         *
*                                         *
*******************************************
```

The <Esc> key enters the information and then takes you back to the main menu. When you inspect this record again you will see that the additional information has been added.

Searching other fields

You must not imagine that a database search is always restricted to just one field. Depending upon the circumstances, different fields will be used to locate a specific record within the overall file. For example if you were examining a library database you would use the author field to find which books by Graham Greene were present in the collection. If instead you were trying to discover who wrote 'Brighton Rock' you would organise your search using the title field as the key and then, if that book were found, look at the content of the author field and discover the name of the novelist.

The possibility of searching other fields is not made explicit by the way the Sinclair Organiser is arranged, but you can search the database using other keys. You are not restricted to the index of the card. This has already been implied by the way the sample database has had specific categories: BORN, DIED, WORK. A search over a wide range like this uses the fifth option on the main menu:

```
SINCLAIR ORGANISER Main Menu

        Recall by Index
             Diary
         Word Processor
   New Address & Cardfile
        Search for data
          Calculator
           Templates
     Exit SINCLAIR ORGANISER
```

When you press S you are given the further choice:

```
        Search data in...

        Address Cards
      General Cardfile
            Diary

       Exit to Main Menu
```

Pressing G leads a request for a specific item. Suppose you pretend you are using the WORK field to conduct a search for April Love. You would therefore add at the prompt:

```
        Search for What ? : April Love
```

The Organiser would then find you the appropriate record:

```
**Cardfile*CardText**********************
* Index HUGHES              Date 23-Feb-89*
*  _____  *
* CHRISTIAN NAMES ARTHUR                   *
* BORN 1830                                *
* DIED 1915                                *
* WORK THE LONG ENGAGEMENT                 *
* APRIL LOVE                               *
*                                          *
*                                          *
*                                          *
*                                          *
*                                          *
 ******************************************
```

Limitations of the Organiser

The fact that you cannot actually define other fields on which to conduct a search is a restriction on the Organiser. Unless you are able to use the index as the key in a search, it has to look through all of the content of each record until it finds the item requested. This makes searching slower than it would be if the amount of information to be checked were limited to only the specific, and fairly small, content of a particular field for each record. Despite this, searching is quite efficient provided that you do not intend to construct large databases. If that is your intention, you should certainly consider purchasing further software. The advice given in chapter 15 should help you here. In any case, the practice given in data handling by the Organiser will not be wasted.

8

Word processing with the Organiser

The Organiser provides a further piece of important software in the form of its word processor. Word processing has proved to be one of the more significant impacts of personal computing in the home, as many people have discovered its advantages over mere handwriting or typing. Once you have become reasonably proficient with the keyboard, you should seriously consider changing over to word processing completely. Give your old typewriter away! Word processed documents look neater and can be easily corrected, if mistakes are made. Naturally you will need to acquire a printer, but the price of these is falling steadily, while the quality of their output seems to become better all the time. A special advantage of word processing is that you will automatically be keeping copies of everything you write as files on disk. Hence you can easily check what you have said in earlier letters sent out. This is cheaper and more convenient than photocopying and does not suffer from the general horrors of carbon paper.

Entering the word processor

The word processor is loaded from the main menu, by highlighting with the cursor and pressing <ENTER>, or by pressing **W**:

```
SINCLAIR ORGANISER Main Menu

        Recall by Index
             Diary
        Word Processor
   New Address & Cardfile
        Search for data
           Calculator
            Templates
     Exit SINCLAIR ORGANISER
```

You will then be asked for the name of the document you wish to see:

```
Document filename :
```

The Organiser will default here to the name of the last document with which you worked. You can press <ENTER> in order to continue with this. Alternatively you may type in a filename for a new document, or ask to see a list of the current documents available. All of this is made clear by the additional prompt which is displayed:

```
Help
Enter name of document Enter document to edit or create & press
Enter.
F9-Show available documents Esc-Exit
To show documents beginning with ''BL'' only enter ''bl'' &
press
F9
```

The Organiser disk comes complete with some documents which you can load immediately for practice. You might prefer, though, to begin typing in something of your own instead. Suppose you decide to try a brief short story. Type in the document filename 'STORY' and press <ENTER>.

Document filename : STORY

You can then begin.

Starting a new document

When you begin a document with the word processor you are given a new window which is slightly smaller than the whole display. You have the usual top line displaying 'SINCLAIR ORGANISER', the 'Safe' message and the date. Apart from this, nearly the whole screen is available for your text. At the top of the window is a another box which shows the name of the document you are typing. It indicates the number of the line and the column where the text cursor is positioned. Everything that you type will be entered, letter by letter, at the current text position and so this is useful information in arranging the layout of a document. The length of the document is also indicated by the 'percentage free' figure, stated at the right hand side of the line:

STORY   Lin 1   Col 1   100% free

You will see this number diminish as you type.

Help is available with the word processor, as with other Organiser facilities. You can summon this at any time by pressing F1:

```
Help
Editing document STORY. Use arrows and editing keys to edit
text.
Esc-Exit Ins-Underline/Bold etc. F9-Show word in database
F4-Recall data
^F7-Window print ^F4-Find/Replace F7-Variable insert
```

You can remove this help window by pressing <Esc> before beginning to type your story.

A sample document

For your initial document, try including some deliberate errors, then you can subsequently practice your editing skills:

```
as he gazed down from the lofty heights of the mountain peke
desmond could still see his chums far below cowering mizerably
beside there tent gosh he thought how did i decide to go on this
great adventure wiv such a bunch of cringing pussyfooting
twerps! desmond waz a dashing sort of chap but sometimes given
to sweeping generalisations any more reflective bloke would
undoubtedly fall vicktim to the superlative charms of irene the
gorgeous blond from quik car taxies plc who had volunteered to
drive the land rover
```

At this point you suffer from the inevitable bout of terrifying self doubt which afflicts any prospective novelist. To overcome this first exposure to creative constipation, you go for the coffee and admit that you might have to exercise a little editorial skill before hitting the bookshelves. This is where the real advantage of word processing comes to your aid. With minimal effort you can soon knock this passage into technical perfection, if, perhaps, not quite yet up to nomination for the Booker Prize.

The editor setup

Before you can begin to correct the mistakes you have made, you will need to familiarise yourself with some of the typical tools for word processing. You can display a menu of these by pressing the <insert> key to the immediate right of the main QWERTY keys:

```
                    Editor setup

        Mode            Insert  Overtype
        Underline       No  Yes
        Bold            No  Yes
        Mark            No  Yes
        Center          No  Yes
```

As always, if you delay in making a choice, further advice is given at the foot of the screen:

```
Help
Editor Setup Change editor setup or text types. Use arrows to
select.
Esc-Accept ^F8-Restore to original settings.
Mode Insert/Overtype typing. Also set Underline, Bold & Mark
(Highlight)
Center will centre current paragraph.
```

When you have made your selection, you return to your document by pressing <Esc>.

Correcting spellings

The more advanced word processors now available have sophisticated spelling checking routines built into the software. See, for example, the word processing packages mentioned in chapter 15. The Sinclair Organiser does not have this enhanced facility. When you are correcting an Organiser document you will need to rely upon your own powers of observation, your ability to spell and your increasing expertise in editing the text displayed on the screen.

Overtype and insert

There are two methods of changing a mistake that you see. If the correct version has exactly the same number of letters as the mistake, then you can select **Overtype**from the Editor setup menu and simply superimpose the correct word on top. It is far more likely, though, that a good proportion of your spelling and typing mistakes will have led to incorrect words with the wrong number of letters. In this case, it is usually quicker to use the insert setting. You can then delete wrong letters and type in the right ones. Actually, this sort of activity is often very much a matter of individual taste. You will probably settle down to your own method of working, perhaps alternating between overtype and insert according to circumstance.

Using the cursor keys

Incorrectly spelt words can be located quickly by using the cursor keys to move the text cursor through the passage. The cursor-up and cursor-down keys move between adjacent lines. The cursor-left and cursor-right keys similarly move from letter to letter in either direction. Combining either the cursor-right or cursor-left key with the control key, <Ctrl>, allows whole words to be jumped, because this key combination is able to identify the gaps between them.

Here it will be assumed that the Organiser has been set for insert. The <Caps Lock> should be left off as most of the letters that have to be typed will be in lower case. When you need to obtain a capital letter you just temporarily hold down the shift key. This is the sensible way to type in a passage.

The first mistake to tackle is the initial 'as'. With the cursor keys you place the text cursor over the letter 'a' and press <Del>. A capital letter 'A' can then be typed in its place. After this the next mistake is 'peke'. Here you can place the cursor over the 'k', press <Del> twice and then type 'ak'. The word is then the correct sort of 'peak'. In the same way you will alter the following: desmond, mizerably, there, i, wiv, desmond, waz, vicktim, irene, blond, quik, car, taxies and plc. Assume that the taxi firm deliberately call themselves 'Quik Car'... The passage will now be:

```
As he gazed down from the lofty heights of the mountain peak
Desmond could still see his chums far below cowering miserably
beside their tent gosh he thought how did I decide to go on this
great adventure with such a bunch of cringing pussyfooting
```

twerps! Desmond was a dashing sort of chap but sometimes given
to sweeping generalisations any more reflective bloke would
undoubtedly fall victim to the superlative charms of Irene the
gorgeous blonde from Quik Car Taxis PLC who had volunteered to
drive the land rover

It still requires alterations for punctuation, slang, sexist sentiments and overall style,
but it is definitely closer to your finished masterpiece.

Inserting punctuation into a passage

It is easy to alter lower case letters to capitals and create the beginnings of new
sentences. It is just like correcting any other spelling error. Similarly inverted commas
and full stops may be inserted where necessary. This gives the further improvement:

As he gazed down from the lofty heights of the mountain peak,
Desmond could still see his chums far below cowering miserably
beside their tent. 'Gosh', he thought, 'how did I decide to go
on this great adventure with such a bunch of cringing pussyfooting twerps?' Desmond was a dashing sort of chap, but
sometimes given to sweeping generalisations. Any more reflective bloke would undoubtedly fall victim to the superlative
charms of Irene, the gorgeous blonde from Quik Car Taxis PLC who
had volunteered to drive the land rover.

Putting extra lines into a passage

It is easy to insert extra lines into a passage, or to begin a new paragraph, provided
that you have set the mode to insert rather than overtype. Simply take the text cursor
to where you want the new line to be and press <ENTER>. For example if you place
the cursor on the initial 'D' of the second occurrence of 'Desmond' and then use
<ENTER> twice, you will find the passage neatly divided into two paragraphs.

Adding a title

Inserting two extra lines at the beginning of the story allows room for a title. After
typing this it is a good opportunity for using the centre text facility. This is selected
as the last choice on the editor setup. First make sure the text cursor is on the line
where you wish to use the facility, then press <Insert>:

                        Editor setup

        Mode   Insert Overtype
        Underline   No   Yes
        Bold   No   Yes
        Mark   No   Yes
        Center   No   Yes

Highlight the 'Yes' on the Center option, then press <Esc>. Type in your title so that the passage will now begin:

```
                    Himalaya Holiday
As he gazed down from the lofty heights of the mountain peak,
Desmond could still see his chums far below cowering miserably
beside their tent. 'Gosh', he thought, 'how did I decide to go
on this...
```

Removing, adding and altering words

Suitable use of the cursor keys and <Del> will let you remove words completely. For example 'bloke' could be taken out of the second paragraph. This eliminates slang at the expense of grammatical sense, and so now 'Any' has to be replaced by 'Anybody'. Provided that the mode is retained as insert, this can also be achieved easily by locating the text cursor immediately after the final 'y' and adding 'body'. Passages can always be altered in this way.

The word processor menu

The editor setup menu is one of the two principal menus you will employ when word processing with the Sinclair Organiser. The other is obtained by pressing <F10>:

```
              Word Processor Menu

                Print Document
                 Import text
              Find and Replace
                Tab settings

              Exit to Main Menu
```

The third of these options will be considered next.

Find and replace

One of the most useful features of word processors is the way in which a repeated section of text can be detected automatically and replaced by another. The overall effect is to produce a nearly identical document, but with vital details subtly altered. Already this is being used by the more enterprising sort of small boy to send out thank-you letters to numerous maiden aunts... Unfortunately a similar technique has become rather notorious in the world of commercial computing, leading to the familiar problem of allegedly personal letters in junk mail.

To use this function, first press <F10> to obtain the appropriate menu and then F. This window will be shown:

```
              Find & Replace

    Find
    Replace with
    Mod            Find      Replace
    Start          Top       Previous   Next    End
```

The further advice given is:

```
Help
Find & Replace Setup Use arrows & editing keys to set Find &
Replace settings
Esc-Accept & do Find/Replace ^F8-Exit without Find & Replace.
Find & Replace starts at cursor position.
```

In the short passage being used, the obvious case of repetition is 'Desmond'. This only occurs twice, but exactly the same process would be carried out in a long document with many occurrences of the same word or phrase. You specify both the target expression and the intended alteration:

```
              Find & Replace

    Find           Desmond
    Replace with   Charles
    Mode           Find      Replace
    Start          Top       Previous   Next    End
```

The mode option should have **Replace** highlighted. Similarly choose **Top** on the last option in order to scan the entire passage. At this stage you press <**Esc**> and are given a final chance to change your mind before the document is updated:

```
              Replace

              Yes
              No
              Abort
           Replace all
```

Selecting **R** will now generate the altered story.

The text altered is not restricted to a single word. Although there is no real need to use Find and Replace to alter a single phrase in a passage of text as short as this, it is useful in large documents. For example, the story can be made less offensive with just a few key strokes:

```
              Find & Replace

    Find           the gorgeous blonde
    Replace with   a Cambridge astrophysicist
    Mode           Find      Replace
    Start          Top       Previous   Next    End
```

This choice will again be confirmed by pressing <**Esc**> followed by **R** at the second window. The current status of the plot is now:

<pre>
                    Himalaya Holiday
As he gazed down from the lofty heights of the mountain peak,
Charles could still see his chums far below cowering miserably
beside their tent. 'Gosh', he thought, 'how did I decide to go
on this great adventure with such a bunch of cringing pussy-
footing twerps?'

Charles was a dashing sort of chap, but sometimes given to
sweeping generalisations. Anybody more reflective would
undoubtedly fall victim to the superlative charms of Irene, a
Cambridge astrophysicist from Quik Car Taxis PLC who had
volunteered to drive the land rover.
</pre>

The Find and Replace option is not the most convenient method for editing a short passage. Nevertheless it could be used here to make various adjustments: 'his chums' to 'numerous colleagues'; 'cowering miserably' to 'making scientific observations'; 'bunch of cringing' to 'band of supreme'; 'pussyfooting twerps' to 'intellectual giants'; and 'Quik Car Taxis PLC' to 'the Institute'. This would lead to the revised version:

<pre>
                    Himalaya Holiday
As he gazed down from the lofty heights of the mountain peak,
Charles could still see numerous colleagues far below making
scientific observations beside their tent. 'Gosh', he thought,
'how did I decide to go on this great adventure with such a band
of supreme intellectual giants?'

Charles was a dashing sort of chap, but sometimes given to
sweeping generalisations. Anybody more reflective would
undoubtedly fall victim to the superlative charms of Irene, a
Cambridge astrophysicist from the Institute who had
volunteered to drive the land rover.
</pre>

Importing text

When generating a new document you can often include other pieces of text written earlier and saved under a specific filename. This is quite a useful word processing technique to develop. Standard passages, which may be useful in a variety of contexts, can be held in reserve and then assembled into quite a long and impressive new document. Naturally, when you do this you will find that a degree of editing may also be required, including the Find and Replace option.

To practice this technique now, you will need temporarily to leave the current document, STORY. Do this by pressing <**Esc**> to return to the main menu. Press **W** to enter the word processor again and then type 'INTRO' as the filename of the new document. Type in this passage:

```
The third expedition to the east face of the mountain was the
one which came closest to capturing an elusive red nosed
shrike, failing only through the oversight of their leader, Sir
Charles Smythe, who forgot to bring the net.
```

Press <Esc> again. At the main menu choose **W** and enter 'STORY' to return to your first document. It will help to enter a second blank line immediately after the title by using <ENTER>. Remember that this only works when **Insert** mode has been selected. Leave the text cursor at the top of the passage in the space formed. Now use <F10> to obtain the menu:

```
            Word Processor Menu

            Print Document
             Import text
           Find and Replace
            Tab settings

           Exit to Main Menu
```

Press **I** and obtain:

```
            Words Import

   Import Format      Ascii WordStar (tm) Document
   Current path
   Import File        Letter
   Extension          DOC
   Fill                No  Yes
```

Further help information will appear at the bottom of the screen as usual. You need alter little on the Words Import box. The default settings are all as you require them, except the import filename. This will always refer to the last document involved. Go to this line and type 'INTRO'. After this press <Esc> to see the enlarged version of STORY:

```
            Himalaya Holiday

The third expedition to the east face of the mountain was the
one which came closest to capturing an elusive red nosed
shrike, failing only through the oversight of their leader, Sir
Charles Smythe, who forgot to bring the net.

As he gazed down from the lofty heights of the mountain peak,
Charles could still see numerous colleagues far below making
scientific observations beside their tent. 'Gosh', he thought,
'how did I decide to go on this great adventure with such a band
of supreme intellectual giants?'
```

Charles was a dashing sort of chap, but sometimes given to
sweeping generalisations. Anybody more reflective would
undoubtedly fall victim to the superlative charms of Irene, a
Cambridge astrophysicist from the Institute who had
volunteered to drive the land rover.

Moving blocks of text with cut and paste

Another of the fundamental operations of any word processor is the facility for
shifting areas of text from one area to another. This is often called 'cut and paste'.
The analogy is with the antique activity of actually slicing up a passage and gluing it
back together in a different order, once a major activity for newspaper sub-editors.

Figure 8.1: Traditional cut-and-paste

The Sinclair Organiser uses keys <F5> and <F6> for this function. In this example
they will be used to swap the order of the second and third paragraphs of STORY.

First position the text cursor on the initial 'A' of the second paragraph. Then press
<F5>. A window does not appear, but a flashing message - 'Show area with cursor' -
is displayed at the top of the screen. Use the cursor-down key to move to the end of
the paragraph. The whole of this will become highlighted. Then press <ENTER> to
see:

```
Delete area
      Yes
      No
```

Press **N** because you do not want to lose the paragraph. Now take the cursor to the end of the third paragraph before pressing **<F6>**. The highlighted area will now be redisplayed here. This happens fairly slowly. Unlike other word processors, where similar block transfer of text is immediate, the Organiser visibly writes to the designated area:

```
              Himalaya Holiday
The third expedition to the east face of the mountain was the
one which came closest to capturing an elusive red nosed
shrike, failing only through the oversight of their leader, Sir
Charles Smythe, who forgot to bring the net.

Charles was a dashing sort of chap, but sometimes given to
sweeping generalisations. Anybody more reflective would
undoubtedly fall victim to the superlative charms of Irene, a
Cambridge astrophysicist from the Institute who had
volunteered to drive the land rover.

As he gazed down from the lofty heights of the mountain peak,
Charles could still see numerous colleagues far below making
scientific observations beside their tent. 'Gosh', he thought,
'how did I decide to go on this great adventure with such a band
of supreme intellectual giants?'
```

File security when deleting blocks

Clearly <F5> can be used as above to mark out whole blocks of text for deletion, which can be confirmed at the prompt which follows pressing <ENTER>, This is useful, but dangerous. Be sure before confirming. The Organiser keeps updating the file on the disk and so you will not have a back-up copy available should anything go wrong. This is not the case with word processors which do not save a document until you explicitly instruct them. One solution would be to create a copy of a document by importing it into another file you have created, with of course a different name. Doing this would mean that you always had a reserve version of an important document in case something unfortunate happened to your current working copy.

Printing a document

If you have a printer attached to your Sinclair PC you can obtain hard copy of the documents that you create. Press <F10> for the word processor menu and press **P**.

```
                  Word Processor Menu

                     Print Document
                     Import text
                   Find and Replace
                     Tab settings

                   Exit to Main Menu
```

The message:

```
        'Printing, wait...'
```

will appear at the top of the screen.

If you try to print when the printer is not connected correctly to the Sinclair PC, this error window appears:

```
                    Problem!
                   No paper
                     LPT1

                     Retry
                     Abort
```

Pressing **A** then returns you to the document as before.

Removing document files

You will not wish to retain all your word processor documents indefinitely. Some may be used again later, but others will merely waste room on the disk. At regular intervals you must decide to have a housekeeping session and remove those files which no longer seem to be of any use.

To achieve this, you must enter the word processor from the main menu. You will then be asked to enter a document name as usual. Ignore this prompt. Instead, press <F9> to see the list of current files:

```
      8 DOC Files                57%Free
   Atempl
   Btempl
   Ctempl
   Letter
   Memo
   Order
   Story
   Wow
```

Use the cursor keys to highlight the file you wish to remove. Pressing <ENTER> at this stage would return you to this document for viewing or editing; to remove the file, press <Del>. This gives the further prompt for confirmation:

```
               Delete file, Sure ?

                       Yes
                       No
```

Highlight 'Yes' and press <ENTER> or press Y. The disk drive will be accessed with the usual reassuring rumble of its motor. On the screen the list of available files is updated to show the list, now omitting the deleted file. If you wish to enter the filename of a new document you are going to work upon, you will need to press <Esc> to remove the list of other files.

9

Looking at MS-DOS

In order to obtain the greatest benefit from your Sinclair PC, it is important to learn as much as you can about the MS-DOS operating system which is provided with the machine. An overview of the function of an operating system has been given in chapter 2, but if the user gains the confidence to experiment a little, this helps to understand the functions of an operating system. At first the various MS-DOS commands will seem rather strange to the beginner. However they are not quite as awe-inspiring as they initially appear to be. Like joining some cabalistic society, it all becomes rather good fun after the first few incantations. It is delightfully easy to impress the outsider. You will begin talking much louder in pubs, and especially at computer shows!

A brief history of MS-DOS

MS-DOS has become such a widely employed operating system that it is hard to appreciate its relatively recent origin. It dates from the time when the computer giant, IBM, at last recognised the growing market for personal computers. At first IBM had held back from entering the rapidly expanding field of microcomputers. Perhaps there was even an element of haughtiness underlying this apparent commercial decision. After all, when you produce a wide range of large mainframe machines, supply companies world wide and have a history in the industry longer than that of any other firm, it is a little demeaning to contemplate home computers no larger than a typewriter. Nevertheless IBM did, eventually, produce an entry for the new market. Their personal computer was launched as late as August 1981. This was four months after the second Sinclair microcomputer, the ZX81. Interestingly, IBM did not write their own operating system for the machine but turned to an outside software house: Microsoft.

William Gates and Paul Allen had been two young programmers who were enthralled in 1975 by the first commercially available microcomputer, the Altair 8800. This machine, which looked nothing like the modern shape of a personal computer but instead resembled a tiny version of a typical cabinet for a mainframe computer, lacked a BASIC interpreter when it was launched. Gates and Allen wrote one themselves for it and sold it to the parent company, MITS. They then went on to form their own firm, Microsoft, and much later were commissioned by IBM to develop the operating system for their new computer. 'MicroSoft Disk Operating System', the obvious name to use, became shortened to its now familiar acronym.

Prior to MS-DOS, CP/M, or 'Control Program for Microcomputers', was the operating system which was used by most microcomputers. This was the product of Digital Research. According to a typical computer industry legend, the contract for the new IBM machine's operating system nearly went to Digital Research, but was frustrated by an untimely holiday taken by the firm's owner. Inevitably, with its overwhelming commercial presence, IBM soon dominated the market for serious personal computing. Following this success, MS-DOS became the new industry standard.

Beginning with MS-DOS - file naming

One of the first things you must understand in your gradual familiarisation with MS-DOS, is concept of the file. A file is a specific program, or a collection of data to be processed by the computer to achieve the desired result. Both the task undertaken, and the end result, depend on the contents of the files, and these can range over a broad realm of possibilities. So that you will know how to keep track of the contents of your files, we will begin by explaining the way in which files are named.

A file name can consist of up to twelve characters, and be divided into two parts: a name (containing a maximum of eight characters), followed by a three-character filename extension. These are always separated by a full stop and so effectively you have eleven characters to select yourself. You do not need to use all of these, and you will discover that many files you encounter possess short names. However as MS-DOS allocates this number of characters it is reasonable to employ them all. Then you can think up fairly explicit descriptions of the files themselves. It is sensible to choose filenames and extensions which will help you remember the nature of the file and what its contents are, at a later date.

Thus some typical filenames plus extensions could be:


```
UNCLE.BOB
FORD.MOT
FORD.TAX
```

One point to note is that MS-DOS reacts the same way to lower and upper case. This means that LETTER.TUE and letter.tue would be completely equivalent to one another as far as MS-DOS was concerned. A mixture of lower and upper case is also identical, like Letter.Tue.

Although you can select three character file extensions of your own choice, there are particular extensions which have a special significance in MS-DOS, like:

.BAT - a 'batch' file

.COM - a 'command' file

.EXE - an 'executable' file

.SYS - a 'system' file

Do not worry for the moment about the nature of these different file types.

The vital MS-DOS files - IO.SYS, MSDOS.SYS, COMMAND.COM

The MS-DOS disk supplied with the Sinclair PC contains a large number of files. A way of displaying a list of these is described in the next chapter. Three particularly significant files are found on this disk, however, which form the core of the operating system. Their names are IO.SYS, MSDOS.SYS and COMMAND.COM. As you may expect, these are program, rather than data, files.

The first two of these are known as 'hidden' files because you cannot see their names displayed upon the screen in the same ready way that you can with other files present.

The IO.SYS file, short for 'input/output', adapts the operating system to your particular computer. MS-DOS itself will run on a wide range of different computers, but because the actual hardware involved varies from machine to machine a go-between is required to make its instructions compatible with the computer concerned. This role is performed by IO.SYS. It therefore needs to be specifically designed for each new model of computer running MS-DOS.

The MSDOS.SYS file provides the operating system itself. In evolutionary terms, it is the closest thing your computer has to the original program written by William Gates and associates, just as your brain stem is reputed to be the part of your psyche nearest to an amphibian...

The third file is not hidden and so you will become quite used to seeing its name displayed on your Sinclair PC's monitor as you begin to experiment with MS-DOS. It is called COMMAND.COM. Its role is to convey instructions from the keyboard to MS-DOS. In the reverse direction it will carry an error message to you, if you type something inappropriate.

The MS-DOS utilities

There is a large number of files on the MS-DOS disk in addition to these three main files. These other files are referred to as 'utilities' and add various extra facilities to the system. Learning how to employ these files for manipulating the contents of your disks is your major objective in studying MS-DOS, as will appear in the succeeding sections of this book.

Booting your Sinclair PC with MS-DOS

The three major MS-DOS files (IO.SYS; MSDOS.SYS and COMMAND.COM) come into action when you first switch on your Sinclair PC. You will see the standard opening screen display, containing, incidentally, one of the fairly rare allusions to the rather confused identity of the company selling your machine. A lot of the domestic history of the British microcomputer industry is tucked away in that initial line!

```
Sinclair PC200 512k (V1.3) (c) 1988 AMSTRAD plc

Please set time and date

Insert a SYSTEM disk into drive A
Then press any key
```

Placing the MS-DOS disk into the drive and pressing a key begins the process of reading the necessary information from the disk to your machine. Initially only a minimal ability to read the disk is held by the electronics inside the computer. It has insufficient information to carry out any tasks yet - all it can do is ask for the relevant data to be fed to it and to receive this information. If the wrong data is offered at this stage, it will be rejected, and a request made for the correct information.

For the moment, ignore the request for date and time and do not concern yourself with the other strange information appearing:

```
Sinclair PC200 512k (V1.3) (c) 1988 AMSTRAD plc

Please set time and date

Insert a SYSTEM disk into drive A
Then press any key

A>PATH \;

A>KEYB UK 437

A>ECHO OFF
Current date is Tue 1-01-1980
Enter new date (dd-mm-yy) :
Current time is 0:17:16.88
Enter new time:
```

The display will freeze each time that the machine expects you to contribute something. Just press <ENTER> until the screen clears to the opening MS-DOS display:

```
MS-DOS Version 3.30
A>
```

The capital letter A, followed by the symbol which looks like a standard 'greater than' sign is called the MS-DOS prompt. It is the computer's way of letting you know that it is now ready to carry out your instructions.

The CONFIG.SYS and AUTOEXEC.BAT files

Two of the MS-DOS utility files have already been accessed by this stage. While the display has been updating itself as shown, a great deal has been going on. A process has occurred through which the computer has rapidly progressed from mere electronics to viable operating system. Like the fabled Baron Munchausen, it has pulled itself up by its bootstraps from the swamp of ignorance to the firm ground of MS-DOS. In doing this the computer has first checked its RAM memory. Then it has looked at the drive to confirm that a 'system' disk is present. It found one of the MS-DOS utility files, CONFIG.SYS, and used this to 'configure the system'. The MS-DOS file was read into memory, as well as part of the COMMAND.COM file. Finally a file called AUTOEXEC.BAT has been checked and any specific commands stored here are carried out.

Internal and external commands

One annoying difficulty which will inevitably arise as you delve into MS-DOS is caused by the distinction between internal and external commands. The problem is especially relevant when you are using an unexpanded, single drive Sinclair PC.

The less frequently used parts of COMMAND.COM are not actually held the whole time in the computer's memory. In order to make room for more urgent requirements, the necessary program file is read into memory from disk when it is needed. This does not cause a problem when a twin drive machine is being used; however, with a single drive machine there is always the possibility that you will not have the appropriate disk inserted when it is required. Unfortunately the screen display does not always prompt you about this and it will have to become a question of experience, or even intuition, to know when you should look for a disk with a copy of COMMAND.COM on it. Regard it as a challenge and a tribute to your expertise. In a somewhat masochistic fashion, frequent disk-swapping does make you feel that you understand what is going on!

Approaching MS-DOS

Learning to use the MS-DOS operating system to your advantage will probably be quite a daunting prospect if you are new to computing. Indeed, you may have only recently been attracted to it by the appeal of the Sinclair PC. Although this machine comes complete with two extremely thorough user manuals, these are perhaps not the ideal starting point. Nothing is worse for the complete beginner than being told too much, too quickly. In order to get the information you require by using MS-DOS, you already need to know quite a lot about it, even before you begin looking!

It is a little like trying to get appropriate details from a telephone directory, especially the more recent copies of Yellow Pages, which seem to become more effusive with every successive edition. In theory, you could use your directory to compile a Christmas card address list, but you must have some idea of at least the surname and initials of your friends. Failing this, it helps if you know roughly where they live in the city or surrounding district. With no information at all about them, a telephone directory is useless, but with just a little initial data you will find that the directory is just what you require.

Similarly, once you have begun to break through into the new territory of MS-DOS, you will find yourself confident in handling the manual and other reference material.

Your Sinclair PC's floppy disks

A computer is essentially a machine which is capable of handling large quantities of information which it processes in the way specified by its stored program and according to instructions given to it by the user. Then it presents the results, usually as a display on the monitor.

The actual data involved simply consist of binary digits, each of which is represented by a one or a zero. Binary digits are often called 'bits', and in this machine, the binary digits are arranged into groups of sixteen. Each group of sixteen bits is known as a 'byte'; a kilobyte (or 'K') of information actually contains 1024 bytes of data, slightly more than the thousand 'kilo' normally implies. Typically, a byte would be used to represent a single character.

It is only because of the extremely large number of bits which can be handled that the overall operation rises above the trivial. It does therefore become extremely important for the computer to have access to a great deal of data. Although the memory on board this particular Sinclair (512K) dwarfs the paltry 1K which seemed quite reasonable on the first Sinclair computer in 1980, it is still not really a very large number in computing terms. In fact all computers need constant access to a 'backing store'. This is a source of further information which, although not immediately in use, is nevertheless close at hand and ready to be employed whenever necessary.

You can draw an analogy with a person shopping in a supermarket. If the customer is sufficiently single-minded, when checking the shelves for baked beans he should be thinking solely about the price on the tin the previous Saturday and, perhaps, about the probable prices in rival stores. That is the data being processed in the cerebral computer. It is only when a tin is selected and transferred to the supermarket trolley that further details are taken from the shopping list in order to choose the next item. The shopping list is here acting as the brain's backing store.

The most common backing store currently used for microcomputers is the floppy disk. The particular sort of floppy disk used by the Sinclair PC is the small sturdy sort, encased in a firm plastic housing. However, just like the more common larger floppies, the working portion is a magnetised plastic disk which rotates inside its outer case.

Its operation is similar in principle to the original gramophone record, where information is recorded as a varying groove which forms a continuous spiral track from the outside edge of the record to almost its centre.

On the modern floppy disk the data is held as series of separate concentric rings, each consisting of a pattern of magnetism corresponding to the one and zero of binary arithmetic. The signal is therefore not continuous or analogue, like the gramophone record, but discrete or digital. The concentric rings are called 'tracks'. A Sinclair PC floppy disk contains eighty tracks altogether. Each of these is divided into nine sectors. Obviously the sectors on the outside track will form a physically longer arc than those on the inside. Nevertheless the disk technology is configured so that exactly the same number of bits are stored in each sector. They are just arranged more closely on the shorter arcs. As the total number of sectors is 9 X 80, or 720, and each sector can hold 1k, one of the floppy disks used by your Sinclair PC can store 720k of information. Note that this is larger than the internal memory of the machine itself.

Their construction ensures that the Sinclair's floppies are fairly secure. Like the old 'Microdrive' advertisement, you can carry them round in your pocket. There is no exposed magnetic surface to worry about. Despite this, however, you must take care of your disks because they can become corrupted. Magnetic fields like those found near a loudspeaker, for example, as well as extremes of temperature should be avoided. The most important safeguard of all, of course, is to make back-up copies of all your important disks. As stressed in the Sinclair PC's manual, this is the first thing you should do with your initial four disks supplied with the machine. The MS-DOS command for doing this will now be explained.

The MS-DOS command - DISKCOPY

DISKCOPY is the command to use whenever you need to copy the entire contents of one disk to another. It is essential that you do this immediately whenever you obtain new software.

Instructions are contained in the manual but here is a recapitulation. You will need to have a new blank floppy disk. Keeping spare disks for this purpose is a good habit to adopt. The instructions which follow assume that you are using the basic, unexpanded Sinclair PC and have not yet installed an additional disk drive. The letter identifying the drive will therefore be A, although this does not need to be used explicitly in this particular case.

First, you should put your disk containing MS-DOS into the disk-drive. This is because the information needed to perform the disk copying process has not been transferred to the Sinclair PC's memory but exists only on the operating system's original disk. This is another example of how a backing store is used to supplement the information in the machine's memory.

The write-protect shutter, the small piece of sliding plastic in the corner of the MS-DOS disk's outer case, must be open. This will prevent information being accidentally copied on to the disk from the new one. At the A-prompt you then type the DISKCOPY command. You must use the American spelling for 'disk':

```
A>DISKCOPY

Insert SOURCE diskette in drive A:

Press any key when ready . . .
```

The 'source diskette' is the floppy disk which you are going to copy. The disk which you will make your copy upon is the 'target diskette'.

Unless you want to make a copy of your MS-DOS disk, remove it from the drive by depressing the release button and then insert the disk which you are going copy. When you press a key on the computer the following further message appears on the screen:

```
Copying 80 tracks
9 Sectors/Track, 2 Side(s)
```

Both green lights will come on to show that the disk drive is being accessed and you will hear the familiar quiet rumble of the drive as it rotates the disk. Information is now being read from the disk into the Sinclair's memory. In due course, the following is added to the display:

```
Insert TARGET diskette in drive A:

Press any key when ready . . .
```

to inform you that the information can now be transferred to the new floppy disk.

This message will actually appear while the drive light is still on. Wait a moment and then remove the disk you are copying and insert the fresh, blank disk. This time the write-protect shutter must be closed, otherwise the computer would not be able to transfer information to the disk. After this press a key, perhaps <ENTER>. The display now shows this:

```
Formatting while copying
```

Do not worry at the moment about this message. It is explained subsequently. Again the drive lights, and noise, will indicate that the machine is occupied. After a further delay the initial message is repeated:

```
Insert SOURCE diskette in drive A:

Press any key when ready . . .
```

Exchange disks and press a key. The rest of the disk's contents are placed in the computer's memory. When this is complete the final copying to the fresh disk is possible:

```
Insert TARGET diskette in drive A:

Press any key when ready . . .
```

When a complete copy has been made, you are given the option of copying another disk. When you make your initial four copies of the disks supplied with the computer you will want to select this choice by pressing **Y**, followed by **<ENTER>**. For this example, however, assume that you do not want to copy another disk and press **N**:

```
Copy another diskette (Y/N) ?N

Insert disk with \COMMAND.COM in drive A
and strike any key when ready
```

At present, do not worry about the technicality of this language. All that this message means in practice is that you must place your MS-DOS disk (or, by this stage, your back-up copy of it) into the disk drive again. Pressing return will then take you back to the MS-DOS A-prompt. Again you will see the drive lights come on briefly as essential information for the operation of the computer is placed back into memory.

10

Becoming confident with MS-DOS

When launching into a new set of concepts and practical techniques, it is important not to overload yourself with too many novel ideas all at once. Psychologically, learning proceeds by a series of small steps. For most people it is unwise to tackle the larger issues all at once. Instead confidence is gradually acquired by testing out what you know already and by practising with simple initial tasks. Only then is it safe to try something more demanding. A particular problem with MS-DOS is the alarmingly thorough way in which the documentation provided with it covers every possible eventuality. Once initiated into its dry, technical world, the operating manual is both fascinating and immensely helpful. However, it does not really try to welcome the beginner.

Once you have used the system disk to boot up your machine, a set of sophisticated instructions are stored as internal commands which give you genuine power over the computer. Additional instructions are also available as external commands on the system disk and can be accessed when required. You can take advantage of the control these commands give you, once you have understood how to organise what you are doing. Sadly, however, MS-DOS can seem very cold and unappealing at first. It does not really encourage the beginner with easily acquired tricks and routines which impress friends without imposing too much mental effort beforehand. To be honest, BASIC programming is the way to feel immediately in control of the Sinclair PC.

Many people new to computers will buy the machine, simply as a result of the low price. As the new Sinclair PC is a 'real' computer, with an industry-standard operating system, it does offer the opportunity to immerse yourself in serious computing. The best way to get the feel of the water is always to paddle before throwing yourself in. Trying out the date and time commands in MS-DOS is a sensible beginning.

The date and time in MS-DOS

When you switch on your Sinclair PC you will be asked to enter the date and the time. You can, in fact, ignore the prompts simply by pressing the <ENTER> key. You will then proceed to the MS-DOS A prompt. However entering the date and time into the machine is a sensible action to take. One particular advantage is that all files you create will be automatically assigned the exact moment in the year when they were created. This can be very useful. Later it can act as a check upon your work, stating when a specific task was completed. It can also indicate, via a little logical deduction, which is your master copy of a given set of disks and which are the back-up copies. This is achieved simply by looking at the date and time information given beside the filename whenever you examine the disk directory with the **DIR** command, as explained later. It is then simple to see just how advanced in their state of preparation the given files are.

Entering the date - DATE

The date is prescribed by the internal command **DATE**. When typed at the MS-DOS A-prompt, followed by pressing the <ENTER> key. The screen display will then be like this:

```
A>DATE
Current date is Tue 1-01-1980
Enter new date (dd-mm-yy):
```

The code in the brackets indicating the way you should type your entry makes its perfectly clear how the new information is required. You type in the day of the month as two digits, then the month and the year in the same two-number format, each separated by a dash. When you press <ENTER>, the screen display then returns to the A-prompt:

```
A>DATE
Current date is Tue 1-01-1980
Enter new date (dd-mm-yy): 18-11-88

>A
```

It would be wrong to suppose, however, that MS-DOS has placidly accepted whatever it was told. Suppose you decide to be frivolous and politely inform your Sinclair PC that it is the 29th February in an inappropriate year. Your mistake would be immediately corrected:

```
A>DATE
Current date is Tue 1-01-1980
Enter new date (dd-mm-yy): 29-02-89

Invalid date
Enter new date (dd-mm-yy):
```

This occurs because the operating system is aware of the distinction that singles out leap years, as well as being able to divide by 4! Of course, if the last two digits of the date do correspond with a 29th February, there will be no problem at all:

```
A>DATE
Current date is Tue 1-01-1980
Enter new date (dd-mm-yy) : 29-02-88

A>
```

You can test the Sinclair immediately and prove to yourself that it really has accepted the date that you have given it. If you have typed in the information above, and then request the **DATE** command again, you will see that this day of the year is now firmly stored away in the machines's memory. You do not need to type the information once more when requested, but can simply press <**ENTER**>.

```
A>DATE
Current date is Mon 29-02-1988
Enter new date (dd-mm-yy) :
```

Note that some additional information has been immediately provided. The computer realises that the 29th February, 1988 was a Monday. This amazing command of the calendar can be tested by selecting some future date from your conventional desk diary and challenging the Sinclair PC to tell you what day of the week that should be. For example, a forward planner for 1990 indicates that the 27th July should be a Friday. The computer can be challenged with this information. Here, the above exchange is continued:

```
A>DATE
Current date is Mon 29-02-1988
Enter new date (dd-mm-yy) : 27-07-90

A> DATE
Current date is Fri 27-07-90
Enter new date (dd-mm-yy) :
```

Occasionally television shows introduce a human with such wonderfully predictive abilities, but for most of us this feat seems quite mysterious!

The MS-DOS ability to test for invalid dates is not simply restricted to an understanding of the calendar. It also rules out other unsuitable information, such as a date well before the advent of personal computing. If you wandered back into the past and attempted the following, you would again be corrected by your Sinclair:

```
A>DATE
Current date is Tue 1-01-1980
Enter new date (dd-mm-yy) : 27-07-71

Invalid date

Enter new date (dd-mm-yy) :
```

The computer does appear really quite sensible about the whole affair!

There are other ways in which you can type the date. You can use oblique slashes rather than the dash shown so far. Again entering **DATE** a second time will show that the information has been accepted:

```
A>DATE
Current date is Tue 1-01-1980
Enter new date (dd-mm-yy) : 11/01/89

A>DATE
Current date is Wed 11-01-1989
Enter new date (dd-mm-yy) :
```

Alternatively, full stops could be employed:

```
A>DATE
Current date is Tue 1-01-1980
Enter new date (dd-mm-yy) : 12.01.89

A>DATE
Current date is Thur 12-01-1989
Enter new date (dd-mm-yy) :
```

It is also acceptable to type in the year as four digits or the month as two.

Remember, when you use the **DATE** command if you discover that the right information is already present, you do not need to retype it in when requested. Pressing the <ENTER> key will inform the machine that you are satisfied with what it has told you and it will return to the A-prompt without any further modification to its position in the calendar.

Bear in mind that the date always has to be set when you begin a session with your Sinclair PC, assuming that you need to know the date for a particular application program. Unlike some other personal computers, the Sinclair does not have internal batteries to keep just enough current passing through the relevant circuitry and allow the computer to remember the date even when the mains supply is switched off.

Entering the time - TIME

A similar command to **DATE** is **TIME**. This requests the time to be typed in the order hours, minutes, seconds and tenths of seconds. The order in which the numbers are to be entered is not made as explicit as with the date. You will be presented with a screen display like this:

```
A>TIME
Current time is 0:02:12:46
Enter new time:
```

You are unlikely to be able to specify the time to the exact second, or tenth of a second. In the latter case the value would change as you were typing it anyway.

Fortunately, MS-DOS does not expect the whole of the information to be given. You could, for example, simply set the hour. If it is ten o'clock at night, type this according to the 24 hour clock. Then enter **TIME** again to check that your value has been accepted:

```
A>TIME
Current time is 0:02:12:46
Enter new time: 22

A>TIME
Current time is 22:00:02:50
Enter new time:
```

It is seen here that typing the hour was sufficient, as indicated by the second value. Note how the time elapsed between entering the two commands also appears on the screen. As before, there is no need to obey the request for a new time if you are satisfied with the value shown. You can just press return.

The value you choose, however, will not be accepted until the return key is pressed. This allows the possibility of setting the time as accurately as you like. If you have a clock or watch you are prepared to trust, or have the radio about to give a time signal, you can type in the appropriate hours and minutes and delay pressing the return key until you know that the seconds is exactly zero. Your method for synchronising the Sinclair PC with the seven o'clock morning time signal would therefore be like this:

```
A>TIME
Current time is 0:02:12:46
Enter new time: 7

A>TIME
Current time is 7:00:02:12
Enter new time:
```

Again a check is shown here that the time has been accepted.

MS-DOS will guard against invalid times being entered:

```
A>TIME
Current time is 7:00:02:12
Enter new time: 7.64

Invalid time
Enter new time:
```

Note however that you do not have to separate hours, minutes or seconds by colons, as suggested by the display. Full stops are an alternative.

Finding your way about MS-DOS

In MS-DOS, everything is held as a series of extremely well regulated and carefully named files. Implicitly, one of the earliest skills you need to acquire is confidence in looking at a disk and finding out precisely what is held upon it. The most immediate way of doing this is to use the command described below. Remember, of course, the possible existence of hidden files on a disk.

Seeing the content of a disk – DIR

Frequently you are going to need to know exactly which files you have present on a disk. This might be after you have made a back-up copy and want to check that all the files are transferred. Alternatively, a particular task may have continued over a long period of time and involved more than one disk. You can find which disk has the most recent version of your work by checking the appropriate filename and the date when this version of it was made.

You can obtain the information which you require through a special MS-DOS file called the directory. This contains a list of all the files on the disk, with the exception of the hidden files. (There is another MS-DOS file containing a list of all the disk's files, but this itself is one of the hidden files and therefore not readily available.) The MS-DOS command which allows you to look at the disk directory, and thus check which files are present, is called **DIR**. Entering this at the A-prompt will immediately cause a great deal of information to scroll rapidly up the screen. In many cases, for example if you request the directory of your MS-DOS disk itself, the first items will be lost completely rather like this:

```
A>DIR

    Volume in drive A is PC200UK1
    Directory of A:\

COMMAND   COM    25276   24-07-87 12:00a
ANSI      SYS     1647   24-07-87 12:00a
CONFIG    SYS       40   21-12-8  12:02p

            [ Further file details ]

RPED      EXE     4644   17-12-87  4:01p
DEVICE    COM     3940   19-08-88  4:40p
SLOW      COM      641   22-08-88  6:54a

        55 File(s)        1024 bytes free
```

There is a way of avoiding this problem. Instead of entering just **DIR** you type **DIR /P**. This then puts the screen display into a 'page mode' and allows you to look at sections of the directory at a time. In order to move to the next page you press a key:

```
GRAPHICS  COM      13943   24-07-87  12:00a
KEYB      COM       9041   24-07-87  12:00a
LABEL     COM       2346   24-07-87  12:00a
Strike a key when ready . . .
```

The way in which **DIR** has operated has been adjusted by adding the optional parameter **/P**. It is now much easier to examine the contents of the disk. You can see that the first two columns of information give the filename and the filename extension. The size of the file then follows and, finally, two columns giving the date and time when it was created.

Other parameters for DIR

There are other parameters which can be used with the **DIR** command. You might decide that you want just the names of the files present on the disk, rather than all the additional information which **DIR** gives you. This reduced information can be produced with the /W parameter:

```
A>DIR /W
```

```
Volume in drive A is PC200UK1
Directory of A:\
```

COMMAND	COM	ANSI	SYS	CONFIG	SYS	
KEYBOARD	SYS	PRINTER	SYS	RAMDRIVE	SYS	
BACKUP	COM	CHKDSK	COM	COMP	COM	[Further details]
DISKCOPY	COM	EDLIN	COM	FDSK	COM	
GRAPHICS	COM	KEYB	COM	LABEL	COM	

[Further details]

Specifying this 'wide' parameter places all the filenames and extensions in five columns across the screen, making it unnecessary to use the /P parameter. After using the wide parameter you can return to the original option for **DIR**, and obtain the additional information, by using the 'long' parameter, **DIR/L**.

Looking for a particular file

DIR can be used to check if a particular file is present on a disk. For example you can see if the BASIC language file, GWBASIC.EXE, is present on your copy of your MS-DOS disk using the instruction **DIR GWBASIC.EXE**

```
A>DIR GWBASIC.EXE

   Volume in drive A is PC200UK1
   Directory of A:\

   GWBASIC   EXE      80592   24-07-87  12:00a
        1 File(s)             1024 bytes free
```

If the file is not present, a suitable message will be given:

```
A>DIR JOKES.OLD

   Volume in drive A is PC200UK1
   Directory of A:\

File not found
```

Wildcards and filenames

An important concept to be employed in all file handling is the idea of a 'wildcard'. It is a technique not restricted, of course, to MS-DOS, or to operating systems, but instead will appear in any area where a degree of random searching is required as found in databases, for example.

Wildcards can be used to replace some or all of the characters in a file name. Two types can be used with the **DIR** command, as follows:

> ? (question mark) – which represents a single character, and

> * (asterisk) – which represents any combination of any number of characters (including no characters).

Suppose DIARY.JAN is the full name of a file which contains personal information compiled in January. Then any of the following wildcard combinations will retrieve it:

> DI???.JAN
>
> D??RY.JAN
>
> DIA??.???
>
> DIA*.JAN
>
> DIA*.J*
>
> D*.*

It can be seen that the number of question marks is always the same as the number of missing letters. Letters can be replaced in the middle of a filename. Only a single asterisk is required for each group of characters removed either in the filename or its extension. However an asterisk cannot be used in the middle of either of them. It must occur at the end.

Note that if you use the * wildcard according to this convention to replace both the filename and the extension (*.*), this can be used to refer to all files present on a disk, since both the filename and the extension can be set to anything. Such a omnivorous wildcard might appear at first to be rather too broad in its application, but it will be seen later than there are applications where it becomes extremely useful.

The reason for employing wildcards is quite simple. It permits you to refer to a whole group of similar files at once. There will be occasions when you do want to do this, as you become more confident in file handling in MS-DOS. For example all your diary files may have these filenames:

DIARY.JAN

DIARY.FEB

DIARY.MAR

DIARY.APR

DIARY.MAY

DIARY.JUN

DIARY.JUL

DIARY.AUG

DIARY.SEP

DIARY.OCT

DIARY.NOV

DIARY.DEC

However using a wildcard you will be able to refer to them collectively, in some file handling context, as DIARY.* and thus make everything much simpler.

Obviously the usefulness of wildcards will depend to quite some extent upon how logical and systematic you have been in your choice of filenames. These must not be randomly selected if the wildcard facility is to be employed efficiently. Some pattern must be established to create similar names for files with similar content. For most people this will be a fairly obvious comment to make, though teachers will probably be aware of the extremely odd names some students tend to choose for their files.

Using wildcards with DIR

An immediate illustration of a wildcard in use can be given. Suppose you want to know what files are present on the MS-DOS disk with the extension EXE. You can use the * wildcard to replace the actual filenames, but retain the extension .EXE. So if you enter **DIR *.EXE** this will give the information you want:

```
A>DIR *.EXE

    Volume in drive A is PC200UK1
    Directory of A:\

    APPEND    EXE     5794   24-07-87  12:00a
    ATTRIB    EXE    10656   24-07-87  12:00a
    EXE2BIN   EXE     3050   24-07-87  12:00a
    FASTOPEN  EXE     3888   24-07-87  12:00a
    FC        EXE    15974   24-07-87  12:00a
    FIND      EXE     6403   24-07-87  12:00a
    JOIN      EXE     9612   24-07-87  12:00a
    LINK      EXE    39172   24-07-87  12:00a
    NLSFUNK   EXE     3029   24-07-87  12:00a
    REPLACE   EXE    13234   24-07-87  12:00a
    SHARE     EXE     8608   24-07-87  12:00a
    SORT      EXE     1946   24-07-87  12:00a
    SUBST     EXE    10552   24-07-87  12:00a
    XCOPY     EXE    11216   24-07-87  12:00a
    GWBASIC   EXE    80592   24-07-87  12:00a
    RPED      EXE     4644   17-12-87   4:01p
         16 File(s)          1024 bytes free
```

In a similar way other groups of files can be listed with **DIR** replacing part of the filename by an appropriate wildcard.

11

Handling your MS-DOS files

You will not begin to feel really confident with MS-DOS until you can begin to handle files at will, creating your own and generally tailoring disks to your specific requirements. Fortunately MS-DOS provides many commands for you to employ and it is merely a question of discovering amongst the various imposing techniques and commands those with which you feel most proficient and which satisfy your needs.

Naturally an early step is learning how to prepare the disks for use. This is achieved with the FORMAT command.

Preparing a floppy disk for use – FORMAT

As well as copying the four disks supplied with your Sinclair PC you will at some stage need to set up other disks for your use. A floppy disk when first purchased cannot be used to store data immediately. Instead its surface has to be prepared with the set of concentric tracks upon which all the minute patterns of magnetic polarity are to be recorded. Think of it as a groundsman putting the chalk lines down prior to an athletics meeting. There is little point in the manufacturer of the disk doing this when the disk is still at the factory because of the different operating systems for which the disk is potentially suitable. Individual operating systems establish a disk's tracks in their own characteristic way. Sometimes it is possible to buy preformatted disks, but in practice this is not a great advantage. In addition to the added expense, it saves little time and care must be taken that the correct disks are purchased.

The MS-DOS command to format a disk before use is quite simply: FORMAT. Before typing this you must ensure that your copy of the MS-DOS disk itself is in the disk drive. The precise form of the command must be correct: the drive letter must be specified, followed by a colon. Only then is the user instructed to remove the MS-DOS disk and place the new floppy into the drive as shown below:

```
A>FORMAT
Drive letter must be specified

A>FORMAT A
Drive letter must be specified
```

```
A>FORMAT A:
Insert new diskette for drive A:
and strike ENTER when ready

Head:   0  Cylinder:   34
```

The number following 'Head' will continue to alternate between 0 and 1 as the 'Cylinder' progressively counts up to 80. At this stage the disk is completely formatted and the last line of the screen text is overwritten to confirm the fact:

```
A>FORMAT A:
Insert new diskette for drive A:
and strike ENTER when ready

Format complete

    730112 bytes total disk space
    730112 bytes available on disk

Format another (Y/N)?
```

Note that 730112, the number of available bytes present, is almost equivalent to 720 kilobytes already stated as the disk's capacity. This is because 1 kilobyte is not actually 1000 bytes but 1024. Multiplying 720 by 1024 gives 737280. The rest of the bytes are used by the operating system.

The prompt requests either a Y or a N key to be pressed. This is error-trapped and so if a different key is selected the message will repeat:

```
Format another (Y/N)?T
Format another (Y/N)?P
Format another (Y/N)?
```

Pressing the N key, followed by <ENTER>, restores the screen display immediately to the MS-DOS A-prompt:

```
Format another (Y/N)?N
A>
```

Selecting Y <ENTER> will allow your next disk to be formatted, precisely as before:

```
Format another (Y/N)?Y

Insert new diskette for drive A:
and strike ENTER when.ready

Format complete

    730112 bytes total disk space
    730112 bytes available on disk

Format another (Y/N)?
```

Although you do have to specify a drive letter, MS-DOS will be quite happy to identify a single drive by the arbitrary one you choose, as naturally there is only one drive to which it can default on the standard Sinclair PC:

```
A>FORMAT B:

Insert new diskette for drive B:
and strike ENTER when ready

Head:  0  Cylinder:  34
```

Again, when the formatting is complete the display returns to the A-prompt:

```
Format complete

    730112 bytes total disk space
    730112 bytes available on disk

Format another (Y/N)?N
A>
```

Protecting your disks

It is extremely easy to pick up the wrong disk when you are carrying out this process and it becomes essential to force yourself to be tidy minded. Even so, errors are possible. As reformatting a disk destroys the information it held previously, an added precaution is built into the disk itself by the manufacturer.

This is the write-protection shutter already mentioned. When it is left open, as it should be on all your essential disks, it is impossible to place any fresh data on to the magnetic surfaces. This prevents information being lost. Naturally it also stops you from formatting a disk. If you attempt to format a disk which has the shutter left open, the computer will soon inform you:

```
A>FORMAT A:

Insert new diskette for drive A:
and strike ENTER when ready

Attempted write-protect violation
Format failure
Format another (Y/N)?
```

At this point you should remove the disk, decide whether it is indeed the one you wish to format and then close the shutter. These problems will tend not to arise if you are efficient in your disk-labelling. The firm plastic cases of the type of floppy disk the Sinclair PC uses are quite readily identified. You do not have the problem of having to avoid writing on the label after it has been fixed to the disk, as is the case with 5.25 inch disks.

Formatting a system disk – FORMAT/S

Disks formatted as described so far do not contain the MS-DOS operating system. They are perfectly adequate for storing programs and data but cannot be used in any context which requires the special operating system files. The only way of placing these on to a disk is to format it with the modified **FORMAT/S** command. This will set up a special system track. The drive letter must be stated:

```
A>FORMAT A:/S
Insert new diskette for drive A:
and strike ENTER when ready

Format complete
System transferred

      730112 bytes total disk space
       78848 bytes used by system
      651264 bytes available on disk

Format another (Y/N)?
```

A disk which has be formatted with the extra system track can be used, just like your MS-DOS disk, to boot the Sinclair PC when it is first switched on.

Transferring system files – SYS

Normally you will add the system track when you initially format your disk. Sometimes, though, you may which to convert an existing disk which contains useful files into a system disk so that you can boot the Sinclair PC from it. This is made possible with the SYS command, provided that there is sufficient room available on the disk.

First make sure that you have your MS-DOS disk present in the drive. Then type:

```
A>SYS B:
```

Note that you are referring to your single drive as if it were the second drive of a twin-drive machine. This is allowed. The display will prompt you further:

```
A>SYS B:

Insert diskette for drive B: and strike
any key when ready
```

Now remove your MS-DOS disk and put in the disk on which you wish to add the system files. Pressing a key will soon update the display to:

```
A>SYS B:

Insert diskette for drive B: and strike
any key when ready

System transferred

A>
```

Naming a disk – FORMAT/V, VOL

A helpful addition to a disk when it is being prepared is to assign it a name, or
'volume label'. This can be a description of up to eleven characters. The command
used is **FORMAT/V**:

```
A>FORMAT A:/V

Insert new diskette for drive A:
and strike ENTER when ready

Format complete

Volume label (11 characters, ENTER for none) ?NOVEL

     730112 bytes total disk space
     730112 bytes available on disk

Format another (Y/N) ?N

A>
```

Once you have done this you can always check precisely which disk you have picked
up. This is a sensible addition to fixing a physical label on the outside. The command
to use to discover the volume label is **VOL** and it results in this display:

```
A>VOL

Volume in drive A is NOVEL

A>
```

If the disk has not been given a volume label, the display will be instead:

```
A>VOL

Volume in drive A has no label

A>
```

Tailoring the display – PROMPT

The MS-DOS prompt which appears each time the <ENTER> key is pressed can be altered with the **PROMPT** command. You simply follow the command with the text that you have chosen and press <**ENTER**>:

```
A>PROMPT MY COMPUTER

MY COMPUTER
MY COMPUTER
MY COMPUTER PROMPT TELL ME WHAT TO DO

TELL ME WHAT TO DO
TELL ME WHAT TO DO
TELL ME WHAT TO DO PROMPT YOUR WISH IS MY COMMAND

YOUR WISH IS MY COMMAND
YOUR WISH IS MY COMMAND
YOUR WISH IS MY COMMAND
```

This can be great fun, but will begin to pall eventually. Do not panic when you try the most obvious way of returning to the A-prompt:

```
YOUR WISH IS MY COMMAND
YOUR WISH IS MY COMMAND
YOUR WISH IS MY COMMAND PROMPT A>
File creation error

YOUR WISH IS MY COMMAND
```

The solution to this impasse is the seemingly improbable sequence:

```
YOUR WISH IS MY COMMAND PROMPT $N$G

A>
```

A useful prompt is the date, achieved with $D, like this:

```
A>PROMPT $D

Sun 15-01-89
Sun 15-01-89
Sun 15-01-89
```

Alternatively the time can be displayed with $T, in this fashion:

```
Sun 15-01-89 PROMPT $T

16:28:59.96
16:29:06.17
16:29:07.21
```

This is far more attention-getting than the random reminders given by radio comperes.

Copying MS-DOS files – COPY

There are many occasions when you will need to copy some of your files. This could be for example when you are setting up a new disk and need some of the files from another to be included. Fortunately MS-DOS has a command which permits you to do this. Logically enough, it has the name **COPY**.

Several distinct variations on the use of copy exist. Probably the simplest is to copy one file from one disk to another without any change of name. Suppose you have the file LETTER.MON on your first disk and require a copy of it upon a second. The standard convention of the names 'source' and 'target' will be used here to refer to these disks respectively.

The most obvious approach does not work. If you are using an unexpanded Sinclair PC with a single drive, you cannot simply type:

```
A>COPY LETTER.MON A:
```

Here you are attempting to instruct the computer to take the file currently located on the disk in drive A and then copy it on to the disk in drive A! This would cause the equivalent of operating system schizophrenia and MS-DOS defends itself stoutly, with a terse rejoinder and another American spelling:

```
A>COPY LETTER.MON A:
File cannot be copied onto itself
        0 File(s) copied
```

Altering your current drive

Instead the only approach is to adopt the rather weird convention of calling the same drive by different names. Pretend that you have spent the extra money and have your second drive, proudly referred to as drive B:

```
A>COPY LETTER.MON B:

Insert diskette for drive B: and strike
any key when ready
```

This the system allows! When the drive stops whirring and the green light goes out, remove your source disk from 'drive A' and place your target disk in 'drive B'. Whistle loudly and hope nobody is looking. Your Sinclair PC feels no shame and goes along happily with the subterfuge, soon confirming that a copy of the original file has been placed on the target disk:

```
A>COPY LETTER.MON B:

Insert diskette for drive B: and strike
any key when ready

1 File(s) copied
```

You can check that the file is present, of course, by using **DIR**. You might as well stop pretending at this point and return to the original drive name:

```
A> DIR A:
```

Your Sinclair PC will still be fantasising about its new acquisition and pretend it is only interested in drive B. It tells you curtly to place the disk back into drive A, even though everybody knows by this point that it has been there all through the copying process:

```
A> DIR A:

Insert diskette for drive A: and strike
any key when ready
```

Assume that you have really done this and just press <ENTER>. You will now see that the file is present on your target disk:

```
A> DIR A:

Insert diskette for drive A: and strike
any key when ready

 Volume in drive A has no label
 Directory of A:\

LETTER   MON   2967    17-12-88   12.28p
         9 File(s)    485840 bytes free
```

Copying files using a wildcard

Possibly you will have a number of files that you wish to copy over on to your new disk. It would be quite a laborious process to copy each one of these individually, but with the wildcard facility already encountered it becomes a far simpler and quicker operation.

Just for practice in using a wildcard with **COPY**, you could try transferring all the files with the filename extension CPI from your MS-DOS disk on to a target disk. Use the * wildcard with the extension .CPI, in the way explained in the last chapter, to form: *.CPI. Your command will therefore be:

```
A> COPY *.CPI B:
```

As the copying takes place, you are prompted each time with the name of the file that the wildcard has selected and also told to exchange source and target disks. This is indicated by the display referring alternately to drive A and drive B:

```
A> COPY *.CPI B:

4201.CPI

Insert diskette for drive B: and strike
any key when ready

5202.CPI

Insert diskette for drive A: and strike
any key when ready

Insert diskette for drive B: and strike
any key when ready

EGA.CPI

Insert diskette for drive A: and strike
any key when ready

Insert diskette for drive B: and strike
any key when ready

          3 File(s) copied
```

This is a very clear example of an occasion when the write-protect shutter on your source disk needs to be kept open!

You can check that these files have been transferred by using **DIR**. Remember that, following the above sequence, your drive is currently going to be regarded as B.

```
A>DIR B:

Volume in drive B has no label
Directory of B:\

4201      CPI    17089    24-07-87    12.00a
5202      CPI      459    24-07-87    12.00a
EGA       CPI    49065    24-07-87    12.00a
      3 File(s)       662528 bytes free
```

Changing the name of a file with COPY

When you make a copy of a file, you can give the new copy a different name, if you wish. When the file is read on to your target disk it will have exactly the same content as the original on the source but be identified by a different filename. This can be quite useful.

Because the files copied in the last section have no special use in the current context, they can be used for further practice. This time you can try changing the name of one of them.

In fact to make the example even easier, you can copy the file EGA.CPI on to the same disk, giving it an irrelevant name. Try ALIAS.WOT. As this file has a different name you do not need to worry about the 'File cannot be copied onto itself' complaint made earlier. All you need to do is add the extra name after the original:

```
A>COPY EGA.CPI ALIAS WOT
```

Note that here you have subtly moved back to drive A. No drive letter needs to be specified because the computer defaults to A. Previously it had been referring to drive B. Now it asks you to insert the disk which contains the file to be copied. Because this disc is already in the disk drive, ignore this instruction and just press <**ENTER**>:

```
A>COPY EGA.CPI ALIAS WOT

Insert diskette for drive A: and strike
any key when ready

1 File(s) copied
```

Now typing **DIR** (without specifying drive A because this has become the current drive) shows that the file has been copied and given the new name:

```
A>DIR

Volume in drive A has no label
Directory of A:\

4201     CPI    17089    24-07-87    12.00a
5202     CPI      459    24-07-87    12.00a
EGA      CPI    49065    24-07-87    12.00a
ALIAS    WOT    49065    24-07-87    12.00a
      4 File(s)       613376 bytes free
```

It has also been copied with its original date. This could be a useful safeguard to prevent dishonest people pretending that they have written something themselves!

Removing a file – DEL

Perhaps you should remove the ignominious ALIAS.WOT before people doubt your moral worth. The command to use is **DEL**. As the current drive is still A, you do not have to specify a drive letter.

```
A>DEL ALIAS.WOT

A>
```

Perhaps a little alarmingly, MS-DOS obeys you immediately without the usual 'Are you really sure you want to destroy this important piece of your program library?'

type of query that you may be used to with more paternal systems. MS-DOS is not always for the faint-hearted. You can prove that the file has been removed by using **DIR** again:

```
A>DIR

Volume in drive A has no label
Directory of A:\

4201      CPI    17089    24-07-87    12.00a
5202      CPI      459    24-07-87    12.00a
EGA       CPI    49065    24-07-87    12.00a
       3 File(s)       662528 bytes free
```

MS-DOS will quail a little if you declare that you want to remove everything from your disk. You can do this using the wildcard * with the extension .CPI or, if other filename extensions are present, by replacing the extension as well and use *.* which embraces every possibility!

```
A>DEL *.*
Are you sure (Y/N)?Y

A>
```

Requesting the directory for your disk will now show that nothing is left:

```
A>DIR

Volume in drive A has no label
Directory of A:\

File not found

A>
```

In this trivial use of **DIR**, MS-DOS tartly refuses to say how many bytes are available!

Changing the name of a file with REN

COPY is not the only way of altering a filename. Another method is to use the explicit MS-DOS command **REN**.

At this stage, if you have followed through the examples in the last section, you will have no files at all on your practice disk. So to provide a file with which you can test the effect of **REN**, copy one of the MS-DOS files across from your main system disk:

```
A>COPY SLOW.COM B:

Insert diskette for drive B: and strike
any key when ready
```

Remember that at this point you remove your MS-DOS disk and put the target disk into the drive before pressing <ENTER>. Use the instruction **DIR B:**, because B: is the current drive again, to check that the file has been copied to the disk:

```
A>COPY SLOW.COM B:

Insert diskette for drive B: and strike
any key when ready

1 File(s) copied

A>DIR B:

Volume in drive B has no label
Directory of B:\

SLOW     COM    641      22-08-88   6:54a
    1 File(s)        729088 bytes free
```

The file can now be given the altered name NEWFILE.TOO. As further practice in knowing which is the current drive, drive B will deliberately not be specified, leading to the request for a disk in drive A. Of course you do not have to move the disk, but just assume that the drive is A and press <ENTER>. The command used for the name change is, as stated, **REN**:

```
A>REN SLOW.COM NEWFILE.TOO

Insert diskette for drive A: and strike
any key when ready

A>
```

No further text is added to the display, so you must check that the name has been changed by using **DIR** again. You do not use **DIR B:** because the current drive is again being called A. The directory will appear and prove that the new name is now present:

```
A>DIR

Volume in drive A has no label
Directory of A:\

NEWFILE  TOO    641      22-08-88   6:54a
    1 File(s)        729088 bytes free
```

After these exercises you should be beginning to feel fairly proficient with the way MS-DOS interacts with the user.

Reasons for renaming a file

REN is used, as explained, to rename a file. This is not just an empty exercise. In general file management there will be occasions when you will need to rename a file. You might later need to adopt a more rigorous convention for your filenames and want to extend this back to your earlier creations. Perhaps various files, which initially did not appear to require grouping together under some broad category, do now seem to belong more closely together. In such circumstances, **REN** will be invaluable.

Renaming with a wildcard

Often you will find that using **REN** with a wildcard might be very useful.

It would be neat if you could fool your future biographer by altering all your diary entries with filenames indicating they were written in 1989 to a set of suitably modified filenames which clearly proved that you had all your most brilliant ideas at least five years earlier! Unfortunately the original date of MS-DOS files is, of course, preserved.

However you might decide to transfer all the letters you have typed during a particular month into separate diary files, According to your personal convention, the letters may all have the same filename extension LET, although the filenames themselves might be quite different. Similarly the new files you will want to create will be given the common extension DIA. This is an appropriate role for the wildcard *, which is used here with the file extensions to give *.LET and *.DIA.

First, display the current filenames on the disk:

```
A>DIR

 Volume in drive A has no label
 Directory of A:\

 GARAGE   LET    12859     3-01-89     3:12p
 VICAR    LET      358    10-01-89     5.23p
 GROCER   LET     1298    12-01-89    11:35a
 UNCLE    LET      375    15-01-89     1:49a
 SCHOOL   LET     3287    22-01-89     4:15p
      5 File(s)       709110 bytes free
```

Use a similar **REN** statement as in the previous example, but include the wildcard as shown. Then use **DIR** to show that the alteration has taken place:

```
A>REN *.LET *.DIA

A>DIR

 Volume in drive A has no label
 Directory of A:\

 GARAGE   DIA    12859     3 -01-89     3:12p
 VICAR    DIA     358     10-01-89     5.23p
 GROCER   DIA    1298     12-01-89    11:35a
 UNCLE    DIA      375    15-01-89     1:49a
 SCHOOL   DIA     3287    22-01-89     4:15p
      5 File(s)       709110 bytes free
```

Combining files – another job for COPY

You can also use **COPY** to combine any two data files to produce a third file. As an example of this, suppose that you want to place your letters to the grocer and the garage together into a new file with a name indicating that both letters related to financial transactions. The filename you decide upon is BILL.DIA. **COPY** is used with the names of the two files to be combined, separated by a plus sign, followed by the name of the new file which is being created:

```
A>COPY GARAGE.DIA+GROCER.DIA BILL.DIA
GARAGE.DIA
GROCER.DIA
      1 File(s) copied
```

Using **DIR** will now show the existence of the file you have just created:

```
A>DIR

 Volume in drive A has no label
 Directory of A:\

 GARAGE    DIA    12859     3-01-89      3:12p
 VICAR     DIA      358    10-01-89    5.23p
 GROCER DIA 1298 12-01-89 11:35a
 UNCLE DIA 375 15-01-89 1:49a
 SCHOOL DIA 3287 22-01-89 4:15p
 BILL DIA 14156 4-02-89 2.45p
 6 File(s) 694954 bytes free
```

Do not worry about the odd byte discrepancy which might appear. Note that the new file is given the current date and time.

As a final piece of tidying, you might decide that there is no longer any point in retaining the two files that have been copied into BILL.DIA. As these are the only ones with filenames beginning with a G they can be removed using wildcards in the following way:

```
A>DEL G*.*
```

Then you can checck the directory to confirm the deletion:

```
A>DIR

 Volume in drive A has no label
 Directory of A:\

 VICAR     DIA      358    10-01-89    5.23p
 UNCLE     DIA    375       15-01-89    1:49a
 SCHOOL    DIA    3287      22-01-89    4:15p
 BILL      DIA    14156      4-02-89    2.45p
         4 File(s)      709111 bytes free
```

Removing a file – ERASE

Another way in which a file can be removed is using the command **ERASE**:

```
A>ERASE SCHOOL.DIA

A>DIR

Volume in drive A has no label
Directory of A:\

VICAR DIA 358 10-01-89 5.23p
UNCLE DIA 375 15-01-89 1:49a
BILL DIA 14156 4-02-89 2.45p
3 File(s) 712398 bytes free
```

As far as the user is concerned, **DEL** and **ERASE** appear to completely remove a file from the disk. This does not really happen, though. All that MS-DOS does is remove the relevant filename from the directory for the disk and indicates that now extra disk space is available for new files. The magnetically stored data are, however, still present on the disk at this stage. They remain there until subsequently overwritten by fresh files. This is why somebody who understands a great deal about what is going on and who is armed with the appropriate software can sometimes recover all sorts of interesting things from a disk which you assumed were lost forever. Nevertheless, it would be unwise to rely upon such extreme measures. It is best to regard **DEL** and **ERASE** as the final act for a particular file.

Sensible disk management – generations of disks

Now that you are able to manipulate files by copying, renaming, combining and deleting them, you will need to keep a careful watch on your disks to make sure that no disasters occur. It would be tragic if, as so often happens, you carefully made a back-up copy only to find out later that you had transferred corruption from one disk to another and thereby lost everything.

Such problems were encountered and tackled long before the invention of personal computing. Industry and commerce adopted a 'Grandfather-Father-Son' approach to disk protection. Forgive the apparent sexist language. The expression has assumed the authority of becoming official terminology and appearing in weighty tomes. If you feel outraged, there is nothing to prevent you, in the privacy of your study, from labelling your disks 'Nan-Mum-Tracy'.

The principle works in this fashion. At the end of a session of working at your Sinclair you will take your current disk containing your files of work and carefully put it on one side. This is the grandfather disk. You find your most recent back-up disk, which is the father, and copy it to the back-up made previously, the son. Finally you return to your grandfather disk and copy it to the father. After that you continue working with the grandfather disk until you stop later to repeat the process. Once you have operated with the routine for a while, it will become quite automatic. It means that should something dreadful happen, and you accidentally make back-up of a corrupted current disk, then you will still have the original back-up with a great deal of your work still preserved. You will only have lost the additional data added during the current session. That you must piece together from memory. The system works quite efficiently unless you are foolish enough not to realise that a disk has become corrupted and thus succeed in transferring the contagion to the third generation. It does have a reassuringly Biblical context.

A diagram will probably help to illustrate how the constantly updated files gradually pass through the sequence of disks. The assumption has been made here that you are at the very beginning of a particular piece of work and therefore begin with no back-up copies at all:

SESSION	CURRENT WORK	GRANDFATHER	FATHER	SON
First	Files'A'	Files'A'	Empty	Empty
Second	Files 'B'	Files'B'	Files'A'	Empty
Third	Files 'C'	Files 'C'	Files'B'	Files'A'
Fourth	Files'D'	Files'D'	Files'C'	Files'B'

How long you choose to make a session before performing the back-up procedure will depend upon how intensively you are using your machine. Certainly most computer users would regard it as being unwise not to make daily back-up copies. If you have achieved a great deal in even a fifteen minute period, then you should treat this as an ideal opportunity for transferring your files down the grandfather-father-son chain. This is especially the case if you have managed to achieve remarkable degree of creativity or otherwise unrepeatable work. Do not make the mistake of entrusting a whole day's work to the vagaries of magnetism superimposed upon plastic. You are bound to encounter an unfortunate loss of data at some time if you are so naïve.

Examining the contents of a disk – CHKDSK

As well as the routine practice of making back-up copies, you may well occasionally want to use the **CHKDSK** command. This will show allocation of disk space.

Because **CHKDSK** is an external command you must first make sure that the MS-DOS disk is in your single drive. Then type:

```
A>CHKDSK B:

Insert diskette for drive B: and strike
any key when ready
```

After this you replace the MS-DOS disk with the one you are checking and press <ENTER>. The display will then show text.similar to the following:

```
730112 bytes total disk space
  3072 bytes in 3 user files
727040 bytes available on disk

524288 bytes total memory
464000 bytes free
```

If you originally gave the disk a label with the **FORMAT/V** option, this will also appear, together with the date on which the disk was created. If the disk has become corrupted in some way, further messages will be displayed giving information on lost clusters and bad sectors. Remember that a sector is a portion of one of the disk's tracks. A cluster is a group of sectors equivalent to the amount of space on the disk that a particular file has required in order to be recorded.

The file allocation table

These losses of disk capacity can occur as a result of physical damage to the disk's surfaces or simply because, in the constant housekeeping performed automatically by the operating system, files have become so widely distributed over the various sectors of the disk that the operating system is now finding it difficult to locate them all. Such problems will be familiar to those people who have worked with Sinclair's earlier venture into the business world. The 1984 Sinclair QL, with its serial access to the minute magnetic tape in its microdrive cartridges, made abundantly clear the way in which this searching process may become unacceptably involved the more a microdrive, or disk, is used.

In order to trace where files are, the operating system uses a special file called the file allocation table, or FAT, but as this is a hidden file it does not concern the user.

Further checking – VERIFY

MS-DOS has the capability of actually checking up on itself whenever data are written to a disk. This is the **VERIFY** command. This can be switched on or off with the commands **VERIFY ON** or **VERIFY OFF**. If it is switched on, it will then report back with a screen message should an error occur during the process of writing to the disk. You can test whether you have this self-monitoring alerted by simply typing the single command VERIFY.

As VERIFY does not produce any comment when there is no error, this implies that the best way that you can practice is like this:

```
A>VERIFY
VERIFY is off

A>VERIFY ON

A>VERIFY
VERIFY is on
```

```
A>VERIFY OFF

A>VERIFY
VERIFY is off
```

Your Sinclair PC's MS-DOS – VER

Do not confuse this last command with a similar one which may appear at first like an acceptable abbreviation. The MS-DOS instruction **VER** informs you of the particular 'model' of the operating system that Microsoft made available to Amstrad/Sinclair when the machine was produced. Like the familiar, though now obsolete, MG Midget and Ford Capri, MS-DOS has reappeared from time to time in a slightly refined new version which incorporates a few improvements, while retaining sufficient of its traditional content to avoid confusion. Prove to yourself which MS-DOS you have by typing **VER**.

```
A>VER

MS-DOS Version 3.30

A>
```

When you are near enough to a friend's alternative IBM PC-compatible, try the same thing and see if you can boast that your Sinclair PC is not just a distinctive colour...

12

Sensible MS-DOS organisa-tion

When you have only a few files on your disks, you will not have any difficulty in locating the ones that you need. All that is required is an appropriate system of names which indicates what a given file contains. However as more material is acquired you will need to become more organised in your approach. You must use a method which ensures that a particular file can be found quickly and easily, without calling too much upon an ability to remember countless filenames.

There is such an file organisation implicit in MS-DOS. It relies heavily upon a concept used widely in computer science. This is the 'tree data structure'.

Family trees and computers

Fortunately the idea of a tree structure is intuitive for nearly everybody. As children we are intrigued by learning about our ancestry. At some stage in our junior school career a teacher will suggest we construct our own family tree:

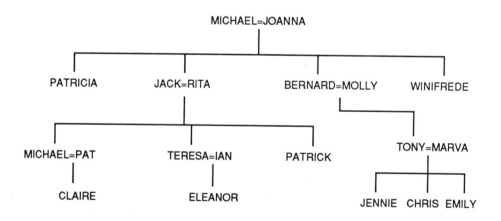

The term 'family tree' itself becomes so ingrained that only occasionally we notice that the tree is, in fact, upside down. The roots are at the top, as implied by the references made about tracing your roots in some other part of the country.

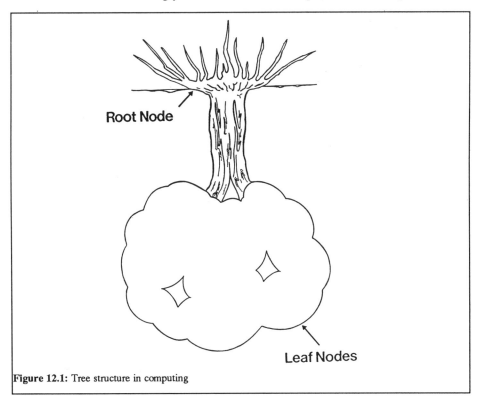

Figure 12.1: Tree structure in computing

When a tree structure is used to store data in a computing application, a combination of both types of terminology is adopted. Sometimes a family tree is implied. At other times the arboreal sort is used as the comparison. This is a little confusing, but the words employed are at least graphic enough to remember. Here is a simple example of a tree structure:

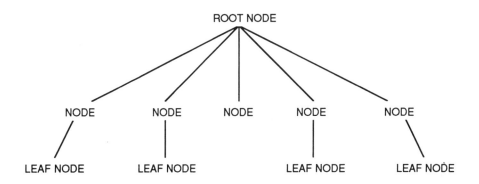

The important point about a tree is that all the 'nodes' spring ultimately from the same 'root node'. The lowest node reached going along any particular route through the tree is called a 'leaf node'. 'Stems' or 'arcs' connect the nodes. All the nodes which originate from a particular node comprise a 'sub-tree' or 'branch'.

At the same time the relationship between nodes connected between adjacent levels of the tree is that of 'parent-child'.

MS-DOS will store its files in a tree structure, but this is not made too explicit in the MS-DOS commands which allow you to control the tree structure being built up. The most obvious reference is to the 'root directory' of the disk's files. This will be explained in detail later in this chapter.

A variety of methods has been devised by computer scientists working in different fields of research to search a tree structure efficiently and find a particular piece of data held at one of the nodes. The whole problem becomes extremely mathematical and an enterprise in itself. None of this need concern you as the MS-DOS user. What you should try to envisage is simply the structure of the tree that you build up to store your MS-DOS files. The operating system itself will handle all the difficult aspects of the problem.

Trees, directories and pathnames

In order to understand the way MS-DOS utilises a tree to locate its files, it will help to consider a third example of a tree. In this the root directory is shown as the root of the tree structure. It is connected not simply to files but to other directories as well. These 'sub-directories', although child nodes with respect to the root, are also parent nodes as far as the leaf nodes, or files, are concerned:

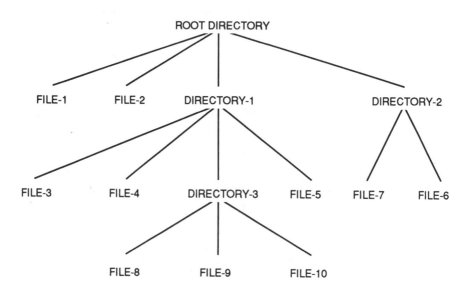

This type of file structure can be examined using the MS-DOS commands specially designed for the task. It should be noted, however, that the tree illustrated here is more complicated than the one used for the initial example of handling directories which is developed below. This example will not exceed a tree with three layers of files and directories.

The illustration does indicate, however, the way in which a particular file can be traced via a given 'path' through the directories. For example the path from the root directory to FILE-2 could be thought of as:

'ROOT-DIRECTORY...FILE-2'

This is different from the 'pathname' which leads to FILE-7, which is:

'ROOT-DIRECTORY...DIRECTORY-2...FILE-7'

Similarly the path which can be traced beginning from the root directory to FILE-9 is:

'ROOT-DIRECTORY...DIRECTORY-1...DIRECTORY-3...FILE-9'

Clearly, each file present in a tree structure will have a unique path to it from the root. This is an inevitable characteristic of a tree structure and is a logical consequence of nodes never possessing more than one parent.

The way in which MS-DOS formalises the idea of using a pathname in order to identify a given file will also be investigated below. The pathnames used by MS-DOS are not formed in exactly the same way as in this example, but the principle is identical.

However before these aspects of MS-DOS are considered it will be necessary to build up a set of files upon which a directory structure can be superimposed.

Simulating a library of test files

Before you can investigate how directories are used, you will need to create a number of files with which you can experiment. Use the technique described earlier of copying one of the MS-DOS files on to a newly formatted disk. Then repeatedly copy this file to the disk, giving it a new name each time so that you build up a selection of files.. These will simulate the genuine library of files which later you will have on a typical disk, although the original date of creation will be identical for each file. An essential point, for the purpose of the current exercise, is that there should be three different filename extensions employed. These will be needed subsequently to illustrate the concept of 'sub-directories'.

First you format a disk, or more probably reformat the disk you have already been using for practice. This time you can attach a volume label, if you like, to remind yourself of the nature of the current exercise. You require the **FORMAT /V** command:

```
A>FORMAT A:/V

Insert new diskette for drive A:
and strike ENTER when ready

Format complete
Volume label (11 characters, ENTER for none) ?DIREC-EX

   730112 bytes total disk space
   730112 available on disk

Format another (Y/N) ?N
A>
```

Now place your MS-DOS disk back in the drive so you can copy one of its files across to your new disk. Here a typical file is chosen:

```
A> COPY SORT.EXE B:

Insert diskette for drive B: and strike
any key when ready
```

Your swap MS-DOS disk for your practice disk, DIREC-EX and press a key:

```
A> COPY SORT.EXE B:

Insert diskette for drive B: and strike
any key when ready

        1 File(s) copied
```

Examining the directory for drive B: now shows what you have so far on your practice disk:

```
A>DIR B:

Volume in drive B is DIREC-EX
Directory of B:\

SORT    EXE     1946    24-07-87 12:00a
        1 File(s)       728064 bytes free
```

At this point you can start building up your library of test files. As explained above, these are going to simulate files that fall naturally into three groups, financial documents, personal correspondence and various files relating to your work. The filename extensions employed here to highlight the three groups suggested, are .FIN, .PER and .WRK.

First copy SORT.EXE to the same disk as an imaginary file about your financial transactions for January. Remember that the current drive is still B, hence the extra prompt:

```
B> a:
A> COPY SORT.EXE JAN.FIN

Insert a diskette for drive A: and strike
any key when ready

        1 File(s) copied
```

Repeat the process to create two further files, FEB.FIN and MAR.FIN:

```
A> COPY SORT.EXE FEB.FIN
        1 File(s) copied

A> COPY SORT.EXE MAR.FIN
        1 File(s) copied
```

Looking at the directory will show what you have achieved:

```
A>DIR

    Volume in drive A is DIREC-EX
    Directory of A:\

SORT    EXE     1946     24-07-87  12:00a
JAN     FIN     1946     24-07-87  12:00a
FEB     FIN     1946     24-07-87  12:00a
MAR     FIN     1946     24-07-87  12:00a
        4 File(s)        721920 bytes free
```

The process is repeated to create the first file relating to personal correspondence:

```
A> COPY SORT.EXE LUCY.PER
        1 File(s) copied
```

In the same way create two further personal files, RACHEL.PER and AMY.PER, and then look at the directory again:

```
A>DIR

    Volume in drive A is DIREC-EX
    Directory of A:\

SORT    EXE     1946     24-07-87  12:00a
JAN     FIN     1946     24-07-87  12:00a
FEB     FIN     1946     24-07-87  12:00a
MAR     FIN     1946     24-07-87  12:00a
LUCY    PER     1946     24-07-87  12:00a
RACHEL  PER     1946     24-07-87  12:00a
AMY     PER     1946     24-07-87  12:00a
        7 File(s)        715776 bytes free
```

The third group of three files, the documents concerning your work, are added in an analogous fashion. Here they are called PREP.WRK, STAFF.WRK and SCH.WRK. The directory will now look like this:

```
A>DIR

    Volume in drive A is DIREC-EX
    Directory of A:\

   SORT    EXE     1946    24-07-87  12:00a
   JAN     FIN     1946    24-07-87  12:00a
   FEB     FIN     1946    24-07-87  12:00a
   MAR     FIN     1946    24-07-87  12:00a
   LUCY    PER     1946    24-07-87  12:00a
   RACHEL  PER     1946    24-07-87  12:00a
   AMY     PER     1946    24-07-87  12:00a
   PREP    WRK     1946    24-07-87  12:00a
   STAFF   WRK     1946    24-07-87  12:00a
   SCH     WRK     1946    24-07-87  12:00a
        10 File(s)      709632 bytes free
```

Finally, to create exactly the set of files required, delete the original SORT.EXE file:

```
A> DEL SORT.EXE

A>DIR

    Volume in drive A is DIREC-EX
    Directory of A:\

   JAN     FIN     1946    24-07-87  12:00a
   FEB     FIN     1946    24-07-87  12:00a
   MAR     FIN     1946    24-07-87  12:00a
   LUCY    PER     1946    24-07-87  12:00a
   RACHEL  PER     1946    24-07-87  12:00a
   AMY     PER     1946    24-07-87  12:00a
   PREP    WRK     1946    24-07-87  12:00a
   STAFF   WRK     1946    24-07-87  12:00a
   SCH     WRK     1946    24-07-87  12:00a
         9 File(s)      711680 bytes free
```

Now you have a set of files which you can use to find out how MS-DOS allows you to impose a tree structure upon your work.

It is important to appreciate that the use of the filename extensions has been adopted here purely for the purpose of explanation. They make it more clear how the different files are grouped together. In practice, of course, if all your work was so tidily arranged you could handle most operations quite efficiently using wildcards. Thus *.FIN would be a convenient way of identifying the financial documents. In a real situation, however, you are unlikely to be able to organise everything quite so explicitly.

The root directory

So far in using the term 'directory', and command **DIR**, the implicit assumption has been made that the main or root directory has been requested. This is simply because it has been the only directory present on the disk.

A logical structure of the current library of files would show each of the files linked to this directory, like this:

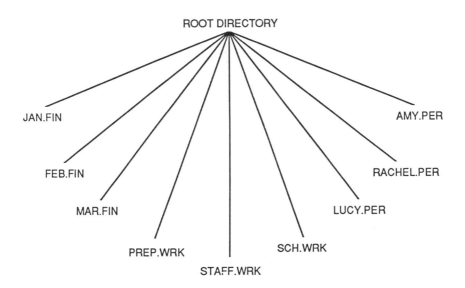

Each of the files is directly linked to the root directory by a single arc. Using the terminology of a tree structure, every node of the tree, except the root itself, is a leaf node. The tree is more like some variety of ground cover plant and certainly not the lofty attraction for birds that can be created using the different MS-DOS commands dedicated to enhancing your file structure.

When you type the simple command **DIR**, with no further qualification, it is this complete file structure that is shown on the screen. All the files linked directly to the root directory are displayed, plus the fact that the system has automatically defaulted to the root directory. This is indicated by the backslash following the drive letter. Perhaps it would be a little more user friendly if MS-DOS explicitly stated the name 'root directory', or just 'root' at this stage, but it does not.

Extending the tree structure

The structure of your files would be far more sensible if the similar categories of files could be grouped together into distinct sub-trees or 'branches'. You would hope to create a tree shaped more in this way:

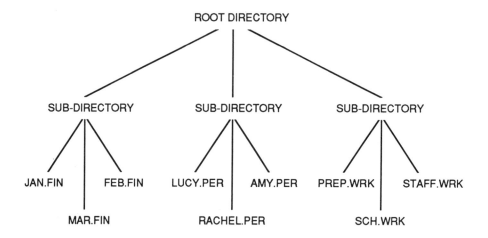

A structure like this is quite obviously much easier to search for particular items. You do not scan at random for the file you require but instead can begin to narrow down the search by looking for appropriate categories and sub-trees. There is no reason, either, why there should not be sub-trees branching off sub-trees, should the files be capable of such further classification.

Fortunately it is precisely this sort of tree structure that MS-DOS allows you to create, using the concept of sub-directory.

Creating sub-directories – MKDIR

You will want to create three different sub-directories to accommodate the three categories of files you have set up on your exercise disk, DIREC-EX. Suppose you call the first of these sub-directories MONEY. Eventually it will refer to the files JAN.FIN, FEB.FIN and MAR.FIN. You set up this new directory on the disk using the **MKDIR**(MaKe DIRectory) command:

```
A>MKDIR MONEY

A>
```

Examination of the main directory shows that MONEY has now been added as a directory file.

```
A>DIR

     Volume in drive A is DIREC-EX
     Directory of A:\

MONEY      <DIR>         18-11-88  12:39p
JAN     FIN    1946      24-07-87  12:00a
FEB     FIN    1946      24-07-87  12:00a
MAR     FIN    1946      24-07-87  12:00a
LUCY    PER    1946      24-07-87  12:00a
RACHEL  PER    1946      24-07-87  12:00a
AMY     PER    1946      24-07-87  12:00a
PREP    WRK    1946      24-07-87  12:00a
STAFF   WRK    1946      24-07-87  12:00a
SCH     WRK    1946      24-07-87  12:00a
        10 File(s)      710656 bytes free
```

In a similar fashion, a sub-directory called FRIENDS can be established. This will be used for the files LUCY.PER, RACHEL.PER and AMY.PER. Again, looking at the main directory after FRIENDS has been created will show that it has been added:

```
A>MKDIR FRIENDS

A>DIR

          Volume in drive A is DIREC-EX
     Directory of A:\

MONEY      <DIR>         18-11-88  12:39p
JAN     FIN    1946      24-07-87  12:00a
FEB     FIN    1946      24-07-87  12:00a
MAR     FIN    1946      24-07-87  12:00a
LUCY    PER    1946      24-07-87  12:00a
RACHEL  PER    1946      24-07-87  12:00a
AMY     PER    1946      24-07-87  12:00a
PREP    WRK    1946      24-07-87  12:00a
STAFF   WRK    1946      24-07-87  12:00a
SCH     WRK    1946      24-07-87  12:00a
FRIENDS    <DIR>         18-11-88  12:50p
        11 File(s)      709632 bytes free
```

Finally add the sub-directory VOCATION, for the files PREP.WRK, STAFF.WRK and SCH.WRK, in the following way:

```
A>MKDIR VOCATION

A>DIR

    Volume in drive A is DIREC-EX
    Directory of A:\

MONEY      <DIR>         18-11-88  12:39p
JAN     FIN    1946      24-07-87  12:00a
FEB     FIN    1946      24-07-87  12:00a
MAR     FIN    1946      24-07-87  12:00a
LUCY    PER    1946      24-07-87  12:00a
RACHEL  PER    1946      24-07-87  12:00a
AMY     PER    1946      24-07-87  12:00a
PREP    WRK    1946      24-07-87  12:00a
STAFF   WRK    1946      24-07-87  12:00a
SCH     WRK    1946      24-07-87  12:00a
FRIENDS    <DIR>         18-11-88  12:50p
VOCATION   <DIR>         18-11-88  12:54p
        12 File(s)     708608 bytes free
```

Transferring files to a sub-directory

You can see which files are held in a given sub-directory by using **DIR** and specifying the sub-directory at the same time, preceded by a backslash (\). With the current status of your practice disk, you should obtain a display like this if you check the sub-directory MONEY, for example:

```
A>DIR \MONEY

    Volume in drive A is DIREC-EX
    Directory of A:\MONEY

.          <DIR>         18-11-88  12:39p
..         <DIR>         18-11-88  12:39p
2 File(s) 708608 bytes free
```

An identical report will be produced for either of the other two sub-directories present on the disk:

```
A>DIR \FRIENDS

    Volume in drive A is DIREC-EX
    Directory of A:\FRIENDS

.          <DIR>         18-11-88  12:39p
..         <DIR>         18-11-88  12:39p
        2 File(s)     708608 bytes free
```

```
A>DIR \VOCATION

Volume in drive A is DIREC-EX
Directory of A:\VOCATION

.            <DIR>        18-11-88   12:39p
..           <DIR>        18-11-88   12:39p
2 File(s) 708608 bytes free
```

These reports show you when the sub-directories were created, and that each one contains two further sub-directories - '.' and '..'These two sub-directories are always created, whenever you make a new sub-directory. None of the files have yet been transferred from the main directory, so the tree structure for the disk will still consist of two levels:

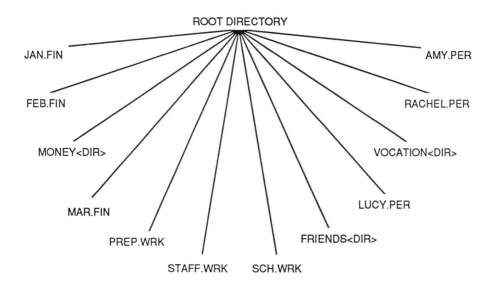

Now, to simplify the structure, you must transfer the files to the various sub-directories and then delete them from the main directory.

This can be achieved using **COPY**. First copy the file JAN.FIN to the directory MONEY. The backslash is used again:

```
A>COPY JAN.FIN \MONEY
     1 File(s) copied
```

This can then be checked by entering **DIR \MONEY** and comparing with the previous result:

```
A>DIR \MONEY

     Volume in drive A is DIREC-EX
     Directory of A:\MONEY
   .           <DIR>          18-11-88  12:39p
   ..          <DIR>          18-11-88  12:39p

JAN     FIN     1946     24-07-87  12:00a
        3 File(s)       706560 bytes free
```

The other two relevant files can also be placed in the sub-directory:

```
A>COPY FEB.FIN \MONEY
     1 File(s) copied

A>COPY MAR.FIN \MONEY
     1 File(s) copied
```

Now the sub-directory will have this display:

```
A>DIR \MONEY

     Volume in drive A is DIREC-EX
     Directory of A:\MONEY

   .           <DIR>          18-11-88  12:39p
   ..          <DIR>          18-11-88  12:39p
JAN     FIN     1946     24-07-87  12:00a
FEB     FIN     1946     24-07-87  12:00a
MAR     FIN     1946     24-07-87 12:00a
        5 File(s)       702464 bytes free
```

Using a wildcard to transfer files

Copying files to a sub-directory is particularly easy if they have a common filename extension, or can all be described via some other easily identified wildcard. If the filenames have been constructed in a logical way, then related files should have similar names. To transfer the personal correspondence files to the FRIENDS sub-directory, you can use: *.PER. If you enter **COPY *.PER \FRIENDS** at the A-prompt you will see:

```
A>COPY *.PER \FRIENDS
LUCY.PER
RACHEL.PER
AMY.PER
        3 File(s) copied
```

If you examine the FRIENDS sub-directory, you will now see:

```
A>DIR \FRIENDS

    Volume in drive A is DIREC-EX
    Directory of A:\FRIENDS

.              <DIR>        18-11-88  12:39p
..             <DIR>        18-11-88  12:39p
LUCY    PER     1946        24-07-87  12:00a
RACHEL  PER     1946        24-07-87  12:00a
AMY     PER     1946        24-07-87  12:00a
        5 File(s)       696320 bytes free
```

Similarly, you can use the * wildcard to transfer your work files as follows:

```
A>COPY *.WRK \VOCATION
PREP.WRK
STAFF.WRK
SCH.WRK
        3 File(s) copied
```

and when you interrogate the VOCATION sub-directory, the following will be displayed:

```
A>DIR \VOCATION

    Volume in drive A is DIREC-EX
    Directory of A:\VOCATION

.              <DIR>        18-11-88  12:39p
..             <DIR>        18-11-88  12:39p
PREP    WRK     1946        24-07-87  12:00a
STAFF   WRK     1946        24-07-87  12:00a
SCH     WRK     1946        24-07-87  12:00a
        5 File(s)       690176 bytes free
```

13

More about MS-DOS directories

At this point it may be useful for you to make a second copy of your practice disk. You will do this, of course, using the **DISKCOPY**command in the way explained in chapter 9. You can then experiment with your library of test files in different ways. Perhaps, to make the following exercises easier to follow, you should label the two disks, say, X and Y.

Put the Y disk on one side and place disk X into the drive. For the present, this is going to be your practice disk. If at any point things go wrong, you still have your original disk which you can use to make another copy, and try again.

The root directory will be as before:

```
A>DIR

    Volume in drive A is DIREC-EX
    Directory of A:\

MONEY          <DIR>         18:11:88  12:39p
JAN      FIN       1946      24:07:87  12:00a
FEB      FIN       1946      24:07:87  12:00a
MAR      FIN       1946      24:07:87  12:00a
LUCY     PER       1946      24:07:87  12:00a
RACHEL   PER       1946      24:07:87  12:00a
AMY      PER       1946      24:07:87  12:00a
PREP     WRK       1946      24:07:87  12:00a
STAFF    WRK       1946      24:07:87  12:00a
SCH      WRK       1946      24:07:87  12:00a
FRIENDS        <DIR>         18:11:88  12:50p
VOCATION       <DIR>         18:11:88  12:54p
         12 File(s)      690176 bytes free
```

Removing a group of files

You can confirm that the correct type of tree structure does exist. In this files will be grouped together under their appropriate sub-directories, and these in turn under the root-directory. To see the structure, it is necessary to do some tree pruning.

First remove all the files with extension .FIN from the root directory by using the wildcard * with the extension .FIN, as follows:

```
A>DEL *.FIN
```

DIR will show the effect of your tree surgery so far:

```
A>DIR

   Volume in drive A is DIREC-EX
   Directory of A:\

MONEY           <DIR>         18:11:88  12:39p
LUCY      PER      1946       24:07:87  12:00a
RACHEL    PER      1946       24:07:87  12:00a
AMY       PER      1946       24:07:87  12:00a
PREP      WRK      1946       24:07:87  12:00a
STAFF     WRK      1946       24:07:87  12:00a
SCH       WRK      1946       24:07:87  12:00a
FRIENDS         <DIR>         18:11:88  12:50p
VOCATION        <DIR>         18:11:88  12:54p
          9 File(s)        696320 bytes free
```

Then use the wildcard with the extension .PER to remove the personal correspondence files, to give this result:

```
A> DEL *.PER

A>DIR

   Volume in drive A is DIREC-EX
   Directory of A:\

MONEY           <DIR>         18:11:88  12:39p
PREP      WRK      1946       24:07:87  12:00a
STAFF     WRK      1946       24:07:87  12:00a
SCH       WRK      1946       24:07:87  12:00a
FRIENDS         <DIR>         18:11:88  12:50p
VOCATION        <DIR>         18:11:88  12:54p
          6 File(s)        702464 bytes free
```

Those old enough to remember the ghoulish American rhyme about a true-life anti-heroine who, 'took an axe and gave her mother forty whacks', thus continuing the pun linking family trees and lumberjacks, can now finish the job off:

141

```
A> DEL *.WRK

A>DIR

    Volume in drive A is DIREC-EX
    Directory of A:\

MONEY          <DIR>        18:11:88  12:39p
FRIENDS        <DIR>        18:11:88  12:50p
VOCATION       <DIR>        18:11:88  12:54p
         3 File(s)          708608 bytes free
```

Making the tree structure explicit

At this stage you have created precisely the tree structure suggested initially. The root directory is connected to the three sub-directories MONEY, FRIENDS and VOCATION. The sub-directory MONEY contains the files JAN.FIN, FEB.FIN and MAR.FIN. The sub-directory FRIENDS is linked to the files LUCY.PER, RACHEL.PER and AMY.PER. Finally, the sub-directory VOCATION is linked with the files PREP.WRK, STAFF.WRK and SCH.WRK.

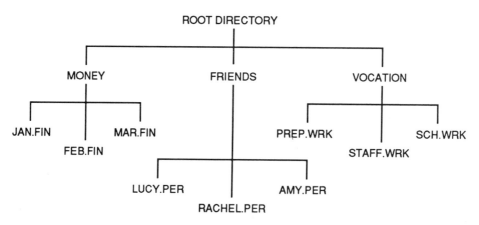

All of this can be shown with **DIR**, using the appropriate sub-directory. First the root directory:

```
A>DIR

    Volume in drive A is DIREC-EX
    Directory of A:\

MONEY          <DIR>        18:11:88  12:39p
FRIENDS        <DIR>        18:11:88  12:50p
VOCATION       <DIR>        18:11:88  12:54p
         3 File(s)          708608 bytes free
```

Next the sub-directory, MONEY:

```
A>DIR \MONEY

    Volume in drive A is DIREC-EX
    Directory of A:\MONEY

    .                <DIR>        18:11:88  12:39p
    ..               <DIR>        18:11:88  12:39p
    JAN      FIN      1946        24:07:87  12:00a
    FEB      FIN      1946        24:07:87  12:00a
    MAR      FIN      1946        24:07:87  12:00a
           5 File(s)          708608 bytes free
```

Note how the other two sub-directories ('.' and '..') are listed here, as they also are in the sub-directory, FRIENDS:

```
A>DIR \FRIENDS

    Volume in drive A is DIREC-EX
    Directory of A:\FRIENDS

    .                <DIR>        18:11:88  12:39p
    ..               <DIR>        18:11:88  12:39p
    LUCY     PER      1946        24:07:87  12:00a
    RACHEL   PER      1946        24:07:87  12:00a
    AMY      PER      1946        24:07:87  12:00a
           5 File(s)          708608 bytes free
```

Finally the remaining group of files is shown under the sub-directory VOCATION:

```
A>DIR \VOCATION

    Volume in drive A is DIREC-EX
    Directory of A:\VOCATION

    .                <DIR>        18:11:88  12:39p
    ..               <DIR>        18:11:88  12:39p
    PREP     WRK      1946        24:07:87  12:00a
    STAFF    WRK      1946        24:07:87  12:00a
    SCH      WRK      1946        24:07:87  12:00a
           5 File(s)          708608 bytes free
```

Revealing the structure - TREE

There is another way of showing the structure of the files you have present on a disk. This is using the MS-DOS command **TREE**. To use this command, you need to put your MS-DOS system disk in the drive and then specify that you want to use **TREE** on the disk in drive B. At the prompt you remove your MS-DOS disk from the drive and replace your practice disk. The display will be like this, although the first part will scroll off the top of your screen:

```
A>TREE B:

Insert diskette for drive B: and strike
any key when ready

DIRECTORY PATH LISTING FOR VOLUME DIREC-EX


Path: \MONEY

Sub-directories: None


Path: \FRIENDS

Sub-directories: None


Path: \VOCATION

Sub-directories: None
```

The second level directories have been shown and, of course, there are no further directories to display, at present. However, we will now demonstrate how you can add third level directories.

Sub-directories within sub-directories

A further level of sub-directories can be created within any existing sub-directory, using the MS-DOS command **MKDIR** However, before you can do this, the relevant sub-directory must become the current directory This is achieved using the command **CHDIR** (**CH**ange **DIR**ectory).

We will create a new sub-directory called BEST within the existing sub-directory FRIENDS and then demonstrate the alteration to the overall tree structure using **TREE**.

First change the current directory to FRIENDS, in the following way:

```
A>CHDIR FRIENDS

A>
```

Now check that you are now in this sub-directory using **DIR**:

```
A>DIR

    Volume in drive A is DIREC-EX
    Directory of A:\FRIENDS

.                 <DIR>         18:11:88  12:39p
..                <DIR>         18:11:88  12:39p
LUCY     PER        1946        24:07:87  12:00a
RACHEL   PER        1946        24:07:87  12:00a
AMY      PER        1946        24:07:87  12:00a
          5 File(s)           708608 bytes free
```

Once in this sub-directory you can use **MKDIR** to set up the additional sub-directory, BEST:

```
A>MKDIR BEST

A>
```

Once more, check the current directory to see that the new directory really is there:

```
A>DIR

    Volume in drive A is DIREC-EX
    Directory of A:\FRIENDS

.                 <DIR>         18:11:88  12:39p
..                <DIR>         18:11:88  12:39p
LUCY     PER        1946        24:07:87  12:00a
RACHEL   PER        1946        24:07:87  12:00a
AMY      PER        1946        24:07:87  12:00a
BEST              <BEST>        19:11:88   3:48a
          6 File(s)           707584 bytes free
```

You could now place files into this new directory, but it is not necessary to do this in order to show the addition to the tree structure. Simply use the **TREE** command a second time, performing the necessary disk changing as before:

```
A>TREE B:

Insert diskette for drive B: and strike
any key when ready

DIRECTORY PATH LISTING FOR VOLUME DIREC-EX


Path: \MONEY

Sub-directories: None
```

```
Path: \FRIENDS

Sub-directories: BEST

Path: \FRIENDS\BEST

Sub-directories: None

Path: \VOCATION

Sub-directories: None
```

The difference to the tree structure is evident. The sub-directory FRIENDS now has the sub-directory BEST, while this itself appears as a separate entity within the overall structure.

Indicating the directory with PROMPT

The **PROMPT** command can be used to show which is the current directory. Suppose you are initially in the root directory and then enter:

```
A>CHDIR \MONEY
```

This makes MONEY the current directory. Type **PROMPT $p** and hold down the <ENTER> key to see how the prompt has changed:

```
A>PROMPT $p

A:\MONEY
A:\MONEY
A:\MONEY
A:\MONEY
```

Using pathnames to access a file

The use of pathnames was touched on briefly in chapter 4, when exploring directory paths. The exact location of a file can be described by stating the path which leads through the tree structure to it. The path begins with the drive name. Then follows any directory name preceded by a backslash and finally the filename itself plus extension, also having a backslash placed immediately before it.

For example, you can construct a pathname to locate your file called LUCY.PER in the following way:

```
PATH A:\FRIENDS\LUCY.PER
```

Altering the date of a file

A rather neat trick can be performed in MS-DOS allowing you able to alter the time and date of a given file. This is extremely useful for Sinclair PC owners, because the absence of a back-up battery means that the date and time have to be set at the beginning of every fresh session of work. In a hurry, you may not bother to do this. Then, to your annoyance, an important file is left with an implausible date and time. Left on its own, MS-DOS will default to some golden era of its own and insist that it is a day in 1980.

This is what you have to do. First, of course, make sure that you have set the time and date to the values that you wish to appear attached to the file. If you are working retrospectively, this will not be the current time and date, and so you will need to fix things again afterwards:

```
A>TIME
Current time is 16:47:37:31
Enter new time: 12:23

A>DATE
Current date is Fri 18-11-1988
Enter new date (dd-mm-yy) : 19-11-88

A>
```

After this you change to the directory which contains the precise file that you wish to adjust. For the file LUCY.PER, this will be:

```
A>CHDIR \FRIENDS
```

You can then check this directory to make sure the relevent file is there:

```
A>DIR

    Volume in drive A is DIREC-EX
    Directory of A:\FRIENDS

    .            <DIR>        18:11:88  12:39p
    ..           <DIR>        18:11:88  12:39p
    LUCY    PER       1946    24:07:87  12:00a
    RACHEL  PER       1946    24:07:87  12:00a
    AMY     PER       1946    24:07:87  12:00a
          5 File(s)          708608 bytes free
```

To change the date and time you use the command **COPY**, but add '+,,' after the filename, as follows:

```
A>COPY LUCY.PER + ,,
A:\LUCY.PER
        1 File(s) copied
```

Examining the directory of the disk now shows that the time and date have indeed been altered, as required:

```
A>DIR

    Volume in drive A is DIREC-EX
    Directory of A:\FRIENDS

    .              <DIR>         18:11:88  12:39p
    ..             <DIR>         18:11:88  12:39p
    LUCY     PER      1946       19:11:88  12:23a
    RACHEL   PER      1946       24:07:87  12:00a
    AMY      PER      1946       24:07:87  12:00a
            5 File(s)           708608 bytes free
```

14

Programming the Sinclair PC200

If you are used to a typical home microcomputer you may be puzzled that the Sinclair PC does not automatically employ BASIC as its programming language. Other Sinclair computers, like the Spectrum, have the BASIC language as an inevitable part of their construction. The language resides on a chip attached to the main circuit board and the user is automatically in a BASIC environment when the machine is switched on. This is not the case with the Sinclair PC. Rather like the early Sharp advertisement, it is a 'clean machine'. You select the programming language you wish to use and insert the appropriate disk. In fact, the Sinclair PC's BASIC is present on the MS-DOS system disk.

You are not restricted to programming the Sinclair PC in BASIC alone. Any language which is available both in a dialect which runs on an IBM PC-compatible machine and on 3.5 inch disks can be used. Pascal is often preferred to BASIC because of its more elegant and precise structure. For those users interested in the field of Artificial Intelligence, LISP and PROLOG are the languages to explore. For sheer mental stimulation, the best language to investigate may well be C. It is all a matter of the individual's choice. However as the language provided with the machine is GW-BASIC, this is the one which is discussed in this chapter.

Beginning GW-BASIC on the Sinclair PC

It would not be feasible to attempt a complete description of a computer language in a single chapter. All that is intended here is a survey of GW-BASIC for those already familiar with BASIC programming. This will highlight differences between it and the other dialects that the reader may already have encountered. At the same time, for those new to programming, it is hoped that there will be sufficient material here to provide at least a taste of what is involved. Only easy illustrations will be given. At the risk of frustrating experienced programmers, the various BASIC instructions included will be briefly explained as encountered. This, together with the reasonably English-like construction of BASIC, should make it possible for the beginner to understand what is taking place. Altering the examples will allow original programs to be written. It is commonly accepted that the best way of learning is by experiment and an interactive language like BASIC is certainly no exception to this rule.

MS-DOS to GW-BASIC

To load BASIC from the MS-DOS disk, you simply type **GWBASIC** at the A-prompt. The disk will be accessed and after a short delay the screen displays:

```
GW-BASIC 3.22
(C) Copyright Microsoft 1983,1984,1985,1986,1987
60300 Bytes free
Ok
```

The 'Ok' is the prompt used by GW-BASIC. It appears cheerfully all the time, even when seemingly inappropriate:

```
GW-BASIC is user-friendly!
Syntax error
Ok
```

Displayed at the bottom of the screen is a list of the predefined commands generated by the function keys at the top of the keyboard. It is a matter of personal taste just how useful these are. A good typist will probably prefer to key in all the necessary commands at the keyboard. At the same time it is a sentimental link with the 'keyword' approach of the original Sinclair microcomputers.

Upper and lower case

BASIC usually expects the user to type all commands in upper case. For example, if you are using a BBC Micro and accidentally hit the key which toggles between upper and lower case, any BASIC instruction then entered will result in an error being generated.

This is not the case with GW-BASIC. As with the version of BASIC Sinclair issued with their QL computer, you can type happily and fast, quite oblivious of whether you have used upper or lower case. As an example, here is a really trivial program which requests the user to type two numbers. Their product is then displayed on the screen. The only two BASIC instructions explicitly required, of course, are **INPUT** and **PRINT**. The former accepts the numbers as variables. The latter places information back on the screen. The program has been entered deliberately in lower case, although English grammar has demanded the single capital at line 30. Note that GW-BASIC is quite conventional in identifying separate steps within a program with an initial line number. The usual increments of 10 are used here:

```
10  input a
20  input b
30  print ''The answer is ''; a * b
```

If you type in a program in this way, and then ask the computer to show you the program listing again, by entering **LIST**, you will see that the conversion to upper case has automatically taken place:

```
LIST
10   INPUT A
20   INPUT B
30   PRINT ''The answer is ''; A * B
Ok
```

The program works just as expected. The BASIC command **RUN**, followed by
<ENTER> is used. Alternatively,key <F2> can be . used.

```
RUN
? 4
? 6
The answer is 24
Ok
```

Loops and data

In the short program just given, some of the words typed in were not converted into
upper case. These were the ones enclosed between quotation marks and forming what
is known as a 'string'. Anything like this will be treated by GW-BASIC as a
complete entity in itself and it will not attempt to alter anything that you have placed
within the string.

Another situation in which conversion to upper case will not be performed is when
data have been placed into a program using the standard BASIC statement, **DATA**.
This is illustrated here with a short routine in which four items of data are first
assigned to the string variable N$ using the BASIC statement **READ**, and then
displayed on the screen with **PRINT**. This is controlled by a **FOR-NEXT** loop,
between lines 10-40. The loop variable employed is the conventional, I, although any
other letter could be used. The program is typed in lower case:

```
10   for i = 1 to 4
20   read n$
30   print n$; '' '';
40   next i
50   data Bertrand, Arthur, William, Russell
```

Once the lines have been typed in, the program can be shown again using **LIST**
<ENTER>. Alternatively, <F1> could be used, also followed by <ENTER>. It can
be seen that the data lines have been left unchanged:

```
LIST
10   FOR I = 1 TO 4
20   READ N$
30   PRINT N$; '' '';
40   NEXT I
50   DATA Bertrand, Arthur, William, Russell
Ok
```

Executing the program with **RUN** shows that each of the four names has been read and then printed as requested. The semicolons, combined with the string consisting of a single character space, both at line 30, result in the names being placed on a single line rather than one beneath the other:

```
RUN
Bertrand Arthur William Russell
Ok
```

An alternative to the extra string at line 30 would be to include the ASCII code for an empty space, 32. ASCII is an acronym for 'American Standard Code for Information Interchange' and is the most widely employed code for representing various letters and numbers. The ASCII code here is converted into the space required by the BASIC function **CHR$**, which yields the 'character string' for a given ASCII code. Note that the value of 32 must be enclosed between brackets:

```
10   FOR I = 1 TO 4
20    READ N$
30   PRINT N$; CHR$ (32);
40   NEXT I
50   DATA Bertrand, Arthur, William, Russell
```

An inelegant BASIC program

Data statements similar to those included in the last example can be easily extended into a very rudimentary data retrieval program. This allows examination marks to be stored together with the names of the relevant candidates. Entering the name of a student will return the score obtained. The program is given here, however, as an example of how a program ought not to be constructed. The use of the two **GOTO** statements, at lines 40 and 50, should be regarded as very poor programming discipline indeed. Free use of this sort of construction soon leads to needlessly complex and difficult programs which can be almost impossible to understand at a later date.

A better way of writing this routine will be illustrated later, but, for the moment, here is the initial listing:

```
10   PRINT ''Type name of person required.''
20   INPUT N$
30   READ A$, B
40   IF N$ = A$ THEN PRINT ''Score is ''; B : GOTO 60
50   GOTO 30
60   END
70   DATA Richard, 37, Anne, 56, Malcolm, 71
80   DATA Bernard, 69, Mary, 42, Jenny, 53
90   DATA Helen, 47, Sian, 85, David, 79
```

The name of the candidate is entered at line 20 and assigned to the string, N$. It is then compared with the known information. The names and scores alternate in the data in a way which ensures that line 30 always assigns corresponding values to the string variable, A$, and to the numeric variable, B. If the current name read from data matches the required name, N$, the conditional, **IF....THEN**, statement at line 40 will print out the score. A **GOTO** in the same line then makes the program end at line 60. Otherwise the second **GOTO** at line 50 is reached and the program jumps back to line 30. It then looks at the next pair of items in data.

Despite the poor structure of the program, it does work:

```
RUN
Type name of person required.
? Helen
Score is 47
Ok
```

Before you become too excited, it is salutary to see the type of error that can occur with a poorly structured program like this one. Suppose somebody who does not know the names of all the candidates involved executes the program and enters a name which is not present in the data statements. This will happen:

```
RUN
Type name of person required.
? Michelle
Out of DATA in 30
Ok
```

Problems like these are avoidable, but first a little interlude is appropriate, to give respite from the ardours of programming.

Ending a programming session - SAVE

The main problem with programming is that it takes up far too much of your time. Successful programmers seem inevitably to be either reclusive or at least fairly antisocial. There is probably no lasting solution for this personal problem except to give up programming, or not begin the activity in the first place. One step in perhaps the right direction is to decide on a fixed time at which your current programming session will end and then stop. Go for a walk, or to bed, or phone somebody. It will prove essential to your sanity.

Simply switching off the Sinclair PC would be inadvisable. Unless the program you are developing is very short and easily retyped, or else hopelessly beyond salvation, you should save a copy of it on disk. In fact, it is best to have a separate disk which is inserted into the drive after you have loaded GW-BASIC from the MS-DOS back-up disk at the beginning of a session. The command which allows you to preserve your work is **SAVE**. Key <F4> gives you this, together with the first pair of quotes needed to enclose the string which will become the filename of your program.

Choose a name. For the above listing, SCORES seems appropriate:

```
SAVE''SCORES''
Ok
```

You can check that your program has been recorded on the disk as an MS-DOS file by returning to MS-DOS using the command **SYSTEM** Then enter **DIR** when the A-prompt appears.

```
SYSTEM

A>DIR
```

A list of all the files held on the disk will appear, but you should see your current program appear as well:

```
SCORES BAS        237   11-01-89  12.15p
```

'BAS' is the MS-DOS filename extension which indicates that this is a BASIC program file. The other information is the size of the program and the date and time it was placed on the disk.

Another way you can see which BASIC programs are present on the disk from within GW-BASIC is by using the command, **FILES**. Instead of returning to MS-DOS, simply type **FILES** and press <ENTER>. All the files held in the current directory will be listed on the screen.

Possible mistakes when saving a program

You must make sure that you are using a disk with sufficient available space. Otherwise you will see this:

```
SAVE''SCORES''
Disk full
Ok
```

This will probably only occur when you forget to replace your MS-DOS disk with your program files disk. Of course, if you have made this mistake but have remembered to keep the write-protect shutter open on the MS-DOS disk, something else will happen. When you attempt to save a program file on any write-protected disk, you will be given this error message:

```
SAVE''SCORES''
Permission Denied
Ok
```

There always seems a note of hostility in the 'Ok' immediately following a rather negative response. You feel you are being hustled.

Beginning a new session - LOAD

When you are ready to begin programming again you load GW-BASIC as before from your MS-DOS disk. Then you must insert the disk of program files where you saved the relevant program from the previous sessions. The assumption is being made here that you are continuing with an earlier program. Even if you are starting something entirely new, you should still insert a suitable a disk for saving your new programs, into the drive.

The command to load your program is **LOAD**, followed by the program file name between quotation marks. If you cannot remember the name from an earlier session, you should use the MS-DOS **DIR** command with the appropriate disk before entering GW-BASIC from the MS-DOS disk. Alternatively, you can use the **FILES** command from within GW-BASIC. Obviously it is considerably quicker just to jot the name down somewhere. When you are programming it is best to keep notes in any case.

The screen display will be as follows. Using **LIST** allows you to check that the program loaded is as you remember it:

```
LOAD ''SCORES''
Ok
LIST
10   PRINT ''Type name of person required.''
20   INPUT N$
30   READ A$, B
40   IF N$ = A$ THEN PRINT ''Score is ''; B : GOTO 60
50   GOTO 30
60   END
70   DATA Richard, 37, Anne, 56, Malcolm, 71
80   DATA Bernard, 69, Mary, 42, Jenny, 53
90   DATA Helen, 47, Sian, 85, David, 79
Ok
```

Control structure in GW-BASIC

The program can now be redeveloped in a more structured way. The essential principle here is to establish precisely what the program is expected to achieve, divide this overall task into obvious subtasks and then code these separately as distinct parts of the program. This logical approach makes any program much easier to understand. Other people can readily appreciate what is taking place. The programmer, too, will find it easier to return later and improve upon the existing structure, extending and modifying it where this seems appropriate. Such 'program maintenance' is an important aspect of computing in both the serious world of commercial and scientific computing and for the amateur.

When beginning such a project it is usually a good idea to start with a flowchart which illustrates the program's operation. The successive boxes of the flowchart often coincide with the distinct subtasks that the programmer will then tackle.

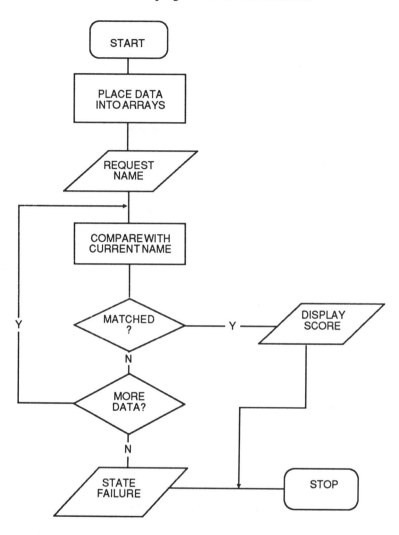

The stages that the program requires are made explicit by a flowchart like this one. A convention exists for the geometric shape of the boxes drawn. The beginning and end of the program are shown by rounded boxes. Input and output from the program are indicated by a parallelogram. A decision is identified by a rhombus orientated with a vertex uppermost. Almost everything else is a rectangle. Other shapes are also used, but these are the most common ones.

Writing program code according to a prepared flowchart will result in a reasonably well structured program. GW-BASIC does, unfortunately, lack certain features which would make it ideal for structured programming. It cannot attain quite the sophistication of the BASIC dialects employed on the original Sinclair QL, or the more recent Acorn Archimedes.

Tidying a program listing

During the modification of the first version of the scores program, extra lines need to be inserted. The jumps of ten in the line numbers allow room for this to happen. If necessary, you can use the command **RENUM** to renumber the lines. By doing this the program listing can be continually updated. Using one of the older BASIC dialects without a renumbering command forced the programmer to think very carefully at the earliest planning stages of any program. Even then tedious renumbering via editing individual lines often became necessary.

A structured program

The scores program can now be shown in a structured form which reflects the subtasks identified by the flowchart. The immediate impression created is of the apparently unnecessary length and resultant memory requirement. This version of the program does, however, have the advantage of being more easily understood and altered. When far more complicated programs than this are contemplated a structured approach becomes essential.

Individual aspects of the listing and new BASIC statements are explained below, after a sample program execution.

```
10   REM SCORES
20   REM A simple database program
30   REM Control routine
40   GOSUB 130 : REM Fill arrays
50   WHILE 1
60   GOSUB 220 : REM Request name
70   GOSUB 270 : REM Search for score
80   GOSUB 370 : REM Display score
90   WEND
100   END
110   REM*********************************
120   REM Dimension arrays
130   READ N
140   DIM PEOPLE$(N), SCORE(N)
150   REM Fill arrays
160   FOR I = 1 TO N
170   READ PEOPLE$(I); SCORE(I)
180   NEXT I
190   RETURN
200   REM*********************************
210   REM Request name of person
220   PRINT ''Type name of person required.''
```

```
230   INPUT N$
240   RETURN
250   REM**********************************
260   REM Search through arrays
270   SF = 1 : REM Set search flag
280   I = 0
290   WHILE SF
300   I = I + 1
310   IF I = N THEN SF = 0 : F = 0
320   IF N$ = PEOPLE$(I) THEN SF = 0 : F = 1
330   WEND
340   RETURN
350   REM **********************************
360   REM Display result
370   IF F = 1 THEN PRINT ''Score is '' ; SCORE(I)
380   IF F = 0 THEN PRINT ''No score found''
390   RETURN
400   REM **********************************
410   REM Number of candidates and scores
420   DATA 9
430   DATA Data for candidates and scores
440   DATA Richard, 37, Anne, 56, Malcolm, 71
450   DATA Bernard, 69, Mary, 42, Jenny, 53
460   DATA Helen, 47, Sian, 85, David, 79
```

A sample program execution

Once the program has been typed in, it should be saved. It is better to save it more than once while you are typing it in, just in case of accidents. Once the program is safely on disk, it can be tested. A sequence of easily remembered names is required.

```
RUN
Type name of person required
? Malcolm
Score is 71
Type name of person required
? Sian
Score is 85
Type name of person required
? David
Score is 79
Type name of person required
? Susan
No score found
Type name of person required
?
```

It can be seen that the 'Out of DATA' error is now avoided. In its current form, the only way of ending the program is to press <CTRL> and <Break> at the same time. This could be altered quite easily if desired.

Unconditional loops in GW-BASIC

The improved structure of the program is made possible by the removal of the unseemly **GOTO** loops and the introduction of a more elegant, conditional loop. There are two examples of such a **WHILE-WEND** structure in the program, between lines 50-90 and between 290-330.

The difference between this type of loop and the simpler **FOR-NEXT** is that the latter has to repeat the number of times stated immediately after the **FOR**. This leads to difficulty in dealing with the varied situations which might occur during the operation of a program. The unconditional nature of a **FOR-NEXT** loop makes it inflexible.

Each time a **WHILE** is included, it has to be followed by a condition. While the condition is true, which can be represented by a non-zero numerical value, the loop will repeat indefinitely. As soon as the condition becomes false, represented by a zero value, it ceases to repeat. This can be seen occurring in a very obvious fashion in the second use of **WHILE-WEND** in the program. At line 270 the 'flag', SF, is set to a value of 1. This represents a true condition for the **WHILE** which follows and so all the program code up to the **WEND** at line 330 keeps repeating. The loop will only end when the name requested is found at line 320 or the end of the data is discovered at line 310. In each case, SF is reset to zero. The condition is no longer true and exit from the loop can take place.

Directing a program with a control routine

The other example of a **WHILE-WEND** loop is at the beginning of the program. Here, at line 50, the condition WHILE 1, will always be true and so the lines 60-90 repeat until you press <CTRL> + <Break>.

This part of the program is a 'control routine' which calls the separate stages of the program's execution as a set of three subroutines. The statement used is **GOSUB**, accompanied by the appropriate line number. What each subroutine is going to achieve is made clear by the inclusion of a **REM** statement on each appropriate line. The **REM** follows the colon which is needed in BASIC to place more than one expression after the same line number. **REM** statements are not executed by a program. They are only included to indicate to anybody studying the listing what is happening at a particular part. In this listing, REM statements are used liberally, including a **REM** followed by asterisks to emphasise where each subroutine is located in the overall structure.

Note how the operation of the program is given back to the control routine by the statement **RETURN** at the end of each subroutine. This is essential for the program's integrity.

Transferring data into arrays

The first of the three subroutines reads all the names and scores of the candidates into two 'arrays'. An array is a common programming data structure and is found in other languages as well as BASIC. It is an extremely simple idea and just assigns a particular numbered location to each item of data. This is rather like sorting out the laundry, taking clothes from the tumble drier and carrying everything up to the bedroom. Just imagine a chest with an unusually large number of drawers, each uniquely labelled and holding only one item of clothing. The next morning you only need to remember associations like 'Blue sweatshirt is in drawer 97'.

Two arrays are used in the program. One holds the names, which is a string array, PEOPLE$, and the other stores the numbers in a numeric array, SCORE. At line 140 it is made explicit how large each array has to be with the **DIM** statement, followed by each array and its size, N. The value of N itself, here 9, has already been read from data by line 130. Organising the program in this way makes it easier to update if new data have to be included, or some deleted. The individual items of data themselves are read into the two arrays by the **FOR-NEXT** loop between lines 160-180.

A very short subroutine

The second subroutine in the program only asks the user for the relevant name and subsequently identifies this as the string N$. Such a brief routine may appear a little pointless, but has been included as a separate stage of the program to emphasise the idea of writing with explicit subroutines.

Organising a search - error trapping

The third subroutine, listed between lines 270-330 performs the main task of identifying the name of the person entered by the user. As already explained, a **WHILE-WEND** loop is used. Inside this loop a variable, I, is successively increased by one at each cycle until the name identified in the array, PEOPLE$(I), matches the one required, N$. When this occurs, the SF flag is set to zero to bring the loop to an end. Additionally a second flag, F, is set to 1. This indicates to the final subroutine that the name has been identified.

This loop can also deal with the situation in which no name is found. This was the problem with the original, unstructured version of the program. In the improved program structure, failure to match the name is identified by the variable I reaching the value of N at line 310. This means that the last name originally stored in the data is now being considered. When this happens, SF is set to zero again to allow the loop to terminate. The flag F is also set to zero, to inform the subroutine which follows that no match has taken place. If this last name does actually match the N$ entered by the user, line 320 can still alter F back to 1 to indicate success. The order of lines 310, 320 is crucial.

Such 'error trapping' is important if a program is going to be easy to operate. The person using it must not be expected to deal with error messages intended for the programmer, like the 'Out of DATA' which appeared before.

The final subroutine between lines 370-390 will simply display the score or a message 'No score found', according to the value assigned to the flag F. The value of I is used to locate the appropriate number in the SCORE array for successful cases.

Making music with the Sinclair PC - PLAY

The above example should have indicated how GW-BASIC provides a pleasant programming environment which allows fully structured programs to be created, even though it does not have quite the sophistication of, for example, BASIC V on the Archimedes. A feature of GW-BASIC, which does encourage the programmer to include interesting 'user friendly' flourishes to a completed piece of software, is the ease with which music can be added.

Traditional Sinclair owners will be familiar with the derision bestowed upon the original Spectrum's **BEEP** command. Almost immediately after the launch of the machine in 1982, this became the target for snide remarks and unfortunate comparison with the much more sophisticated musical capabilities of the rival Acorn/BBC computer. This defect was engineered out of the later Spectrum design and similarly the new Sinclair PC has also made up for any of the deficiencies of its distant ancestor. The inclusion of the command **PLAY** permits snatches of music to be included wherever the programmer feels is relevant.

PLAY is followed by a string constant, a series of characters enclosed in quotes. Notes of the octave are represented by their conventional letters. The octave required is defined by the letter O, followed by a number from 0 to 6. For example, in this illustration of the Sinclair's **PLAY** statement, the string contains the notes necessary for the nursery rhyme 'There was a pig':

```
10 PLAY ''O1AO2DEFGAO3DO2D''
```

An almost equally brief program places the same musical information as a data statement which is then read as the string A$ before being operated upon by **PLAY**:

```
10   READ A$
20   PLAY A$
30   DATA O1AO2DEFGAO3DO2D
```

This approach allows more flexibility within a program. You might want to introduce a number of different tunes into, perhaps, a game, each played at various stages of the operation of the program. All that would then be required would be to code the music as data statements and then use the instruction **RESTORE**, followed by the appropriate line number, to set the 'data pointer' at the correct information before using **PLAY**. Here is an example of the type of routine required. Note the 'empty' loop providing a delay between the two parts of the tune at line 50:

```
10   RESTORE 70
20   FOR I = 1 TO 2
30   READ A$
40   PLAY A$
50   FOR T = 1 TO 1000 : NEXT T
60   NEXT I
70   DATA O1AO2DEFGAO3DO2D
80   DATA MSO1AO2DEFGAO3DO2D
```

Another effect possible has been indicated by the MS included at the beginning of the data in line 80. This is the 'music staccato' code. Various possibilities like this are detailed in the GW-BASIC user guide provided with the Sinclair PC.

Drawing with GW-BASIC - SCREEN and LINE

A major difference between the various dialects of BASIC provided with microcomputers is the way in which they handle graphics output to the screen. GW-BASIC allows quite subtle effects to be created. Two important instructions are **SCREEN** and **LINE**. The former selects an appropriate graphics mode and the second allows lines to be drawn between coordinate points on the screen. As a simple example of this command, the following program constructs a pyramid with vertices at points (320,20), (120,180), (520,180) and (550,110).

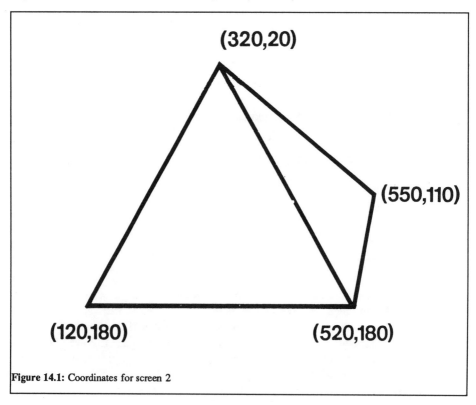

Figure 14.1: Coordinates for screen 2

The structure of the program is very similar to the earlier example. It uses a single **FOR-NEXT** loop reading the coordinate information from data statements. Each line is identified by the coordinates of its beginning, (A,B), and its end, (C,D). These are first acquired from the data statements by **READ**, at line 50, and then joined on the screen by the **LINE** statement at 60. The total number of lines in the picture, in this case 5, is coded as the initial item of data and then used to control the number of times that the loop repeats:

```
10   SCREEN 2
20   CLS
30   READ N
40   FOR I = 1 TO N
50   READ A,B,C,D
60   LINE (A,B) - (C,D)
70   NEXT I
80   DATA  5
90   DATA 120, 180, 520, 180
100   DATA 120, 180, 320, 20
110   DATA 320, 20, 520, 180
120   DATA 520, 180, 550, 110
130   DATA 320, 20, 550, 110
```

Although the program is quite elementary, it does begin to show the type of effect possible with the graphics included in GW-BASIC. The duplication of coordinate points seen in the data statements could be avoided by a routine which drew the shape in a continuous fashion. The advantage of the current routine is the ease with which any shape can be drawn by simply providing different data. The main body of the program remains the same.

15

Choosing application software

The Sinclair PC200 provides a remarkable degree of value for its price. The purchaser obtains a fully compatible IBM clone with an 8 Megahertz, sixteen-bit processor and 512 Kilobytes of RAM. This combined with the machine's inherent potential for expansion makes it a very serious addition to the home. The Organiser software provided shows immediately the type of work that the computer can handle and undoubtedly will prove sufficient for most people's needs.

Nevertheless, having made the investment in the Sinclair PC200, it would be unwise not to consider at a later stage the way in which the machine's usefulness could be extended still further. Sinclair Organiser should have shown you the type of information processing that you can use a computer to help you with. It is simply a question then of deciding precisely which of the available packages best suit your individual requirements.

The most obvious types business software to consider are word processing packages, spreadsheets and databases. Other possibilities include electronic mail and graphics software. Obviously having saved money in your initial purchase of the Sinclair PC, you will not wish to spend too much by acquiring some of the more expensive programs currently available. In fact, you may decide to cut expenditure to a minimum by looking out for a suitable suite of integrated software.

Integrated business software

One of the traditional problems in computing has been the lack of compatibility between different computers. Users of business systems have quite justifiably complained that the whole purpose of introducing computers into the workplace is to make life easier. They argue that being unable to transfer data from one system to another is an unnecessary complication. Sadly, such incompatibility has extended even into the realm of software. You will discover that different pieces of work carried out on the same machine, with data stored on apparently identical floppy disks, might not be easily combined into an overall finished item. You might have details of clients' accounts held in your database. When you use your word processor to compose a relevant document referring to this information you, quite reasonably expect to be able to incorporate some of it into your work. Unfortunately you then

164

discover that this is not possible. The datafiles compiled by one piece of software will not be easily accessed, under user control, by another. You find yourself either consulting an expert or, to save time, retyping the relevant information back from the hardcopy produced by the database on to the screen display of the word processor. This hardly qualifies for the much heralded 'electronic office'.

Fortunately software houses have seen the need to resolve this problem. There are now a number of 'integrated' software packages available in which separate types of traditional business program are combined into an overall piece of software. A typical integrated package will contain a word processor, spreadsheet and database. Files from one are immediately available to the others. Thus you might extract information from the database, perform various calculations using this information on a spreadsheet, and then transfer some of the results into a document being generated by the word processor.

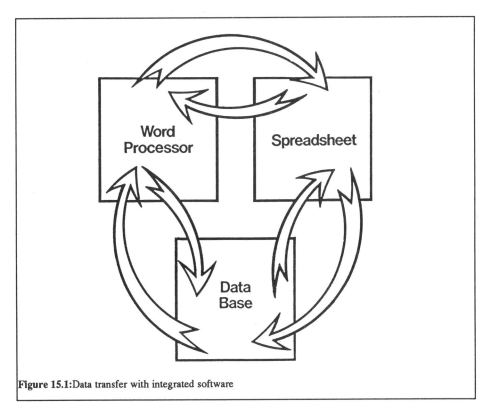

Figure 15.1: Data transfer with integrated software

The major advantage of such a piece of software is the ready transfer of data from one application to another. An incidental additional advantage, of course, is that usually there is a cost saving. The purchase price of separate word processor, spreadsheet and database is likely to exceed the combined price of an equivalent integrated suite.

Other facilities besides the three already mentioned are also available with a good integrated package, but inevitably these more sophisticated packages do require the more powerful personal computers now available. For example if you had purchased one of the Sinclair PC's big brothers, the PC2000 series, incidentally introduced to the London public at the same Earls Court computer show, you would be able to use a very powerful integrated package, like MicroSoft's Excel. The advanced 80286 and 80386 processors employed with these computers, together with their one and four Megabyte memories, permit far more to be achieved in the design of the integrated package. Microsoft's Excel, for example, is able to utilise the windows facility developed by Microsoft, which makes screen displays far more comprehensive. It can also generate elaborate graphics, for both display and printer, and provide detailed on-line help and instruction for the user. Other refinements involve extension of the power of the word processor, spreadsheet and database themselves. Entry into a spreadsheet is automatically monitored to prevent unnecessary recalculation of values, for example, and multiple levels of spreadsheet can be 'stacked' to increase their potential still further.

The Sinclair PC cannot run an integrated package of this power but there are perfectly suitable packages available for the machine. These will be considered later in this chapter, and one in some detail. First, however, some of the other serious business software will be briefly investigated. A more comprehensive explanation of some of the concepts introduced will, of course, be found in the final sections devoted to the integrated software.

Cheap word processing

Using the word processing component of Sinclair Organiser will have given some indication of the power of a word processor. It is not really adequate, however, for extensive work in this area. Any Sinclair PC owner who wishes to obtain the maximum satisfaction from the computer will need to consider buying one of the other word processors currently available.

One possibility, as already stated, would be to buy an integrated package and employ the word processor resident in that. This will be considered later. If, though, word processing is the only facility required, it will be necessary to look at the individual word processor programs produced by different software houses.

A typical example of a word processor is PC Write. This is a program from Sagesoft Limited, NEI House,Regent Centre, Gosforth, Newcastle upon Tyne. (Telephone 091-213-1555). Earlier versions are available from suppliers of shareware software.

Although intended to be an easy introduction to word processing, at the same time PC Write does not leave out the sort of features that an experienced user would expect to find. It can operate in conjunction with a variety of different printers because it includes the necessary 'printer drivers' as part of the program. A 45-thousand word spelling checker is included, as well as an original split screen facility which permits two separate files to be edited at the same time. Like many .of the better word processors, it also contains on-line help boxes, which can be called upon when the person using the software is uncertain about how to proceed further.

PC Write is issued with a very full manual which includes a comprehensive tutorial guide.

Remember that you will need to consult your dealer in order to make the correct final decision about such software. Though many software packages will operate perfectly adequately with the single drive, unexpanded Sinclair PC, it is indisputable that the more you use a particular program the more you may feel that the extra cost of a second drive is easily justified by the increased economy of time. The constant disk swapping inevitable with a single drive can become quite irritating.

Usually you need to follow an installation procedure before the software will run at all. It is at this stage you will need your dealer's advice about single or twin drives.

Buying a spreadsheet

A good spreadsheet program will be needed by anybody who intends to perform financial or mathematical work with their Sinclair PC. As described in more detail subsequently, a spreadsheet allows various calculations to be performed upon the cross-referenced contents of its individual 'cells'.

Good value for money is provided by Sage's PC Planner. This has been designed to allow users practical experience which many later help them should they encounter the business-standard spreadsheet software, Lotus 1-2-3. PC Planner is controlled through a clear menu, which permits the user easy access to the software's many features. This is especially appropriate when graphics are being generated from the results obtained with a particular spreadsheet. Two levels of graphical work are possible, level one will allow simple graphs to be constructed from initial data, then level two builds upon this to generate a sufficiently colourful and presentable final result.

The spreadsheet can contain up to 2047 cells, which is adequate most conceivable applications. The macro language facility provided also allows for complicated sets of manipulations to be programmed for operation on the cell contents.

A relational database

The third standard piece of business software is a good database. Sage's Retrieve III comes into this category. It is a relational database which permits easier interrogation than a hierarchical system because the relations between items of information are reasserted as queries are made, rather than being established permanently when the data are first added to the system.

Retrieve III is a powerful system suitable for various applications, like stock control, staff records, invoicing and, of course, purely personal and domestic data handling.

It has an original method for designing data entry screens which allows the user considerable freedom. Colours and even simple graphics are possible.

Communications software

The Sinclair PC has the potential for adding a modem card in one of the expansion slots. If the user does eventually follow this path, suitable communications software will become essential. Sagesoft is particularly proud of its Chit-Chat software, which won a British Microcomputing Award for best communications software.

Installing a modem and purchasing Chit-Chat will introduce the Sinclair PC to the world of electronic mail. Messages from the user's Sinclair PC will be received by a central computer and stored in the electronic equivalent of a pigeon hole, capable of being accessed by the recipient alone. Obviously this is only going to be a significant advantage only for those people with plenty of friends with the same attitude towards the modern technological culture. Another disadvantage, naturally, is the ease with which colossal phone bills can be created. Nevertheless the sensible use of the facility cannot be denied. There are various electronic mail services currently available, like Telecom Gold and One-to-One. Details of subscribing to these networks are easily obtained.

Sage's Chit-Chat also allows access to Prestel and other viewdata services. For those with a meteorological bent, or perhaps just the frustrated astronaut, it is also becoming possible to receive satellite images from space, although obviously it would be necessary to make the relevant enquiries first into the feasibility of such a marvel.

The home accountant

The negative image conferred upon accountancy by Monty Python is probably best resolved by an efficient accountancy package. Thus armed it should be possible to use your word processor to devise countless reasons 'why accountancy is not boring'.

Sage's Payroll II is entirely suitable for the small business. It can handle pay calculations and generate reports. It is knowledgeable about UK tax codes and permits ready post-budget alterations to its internal data. Various adjustments are possible to individual payslip details and the package is even capable of dealing with pension contributions.

An integrated package

An excellent integrated package for personal computers is Ability, available from Migent (UK) Limited at 37 Dover Street, London, W1X 3RB. (Telephone 01 493 2655). It consists of two versions, the earlier, Ability, is currently sold for under £100. The extended Ability Plus is more expensive, though still considerably less than £200, and pushes the Sinclair PC to its limit. It certainly requires an expanded machine with two drives and even then may prove difficult to use because of memory requirements.

Ability supports a relational database. Information is typed in very much as if the user was employing the word processor, with the distinction that the various fields for the different categories of information are also present. Two separate files held in the system can always be linked via a common field, though of course the fully relational facility will go well beyond this.

The word processor has a full 'what you see is what you get' (wysiwyg) display, a boon for anybody who has been obliged to work with the unrealistic screen displays usually accompanying word processors intended to be used in schools. The Ability Plus version has a 148-thousand word spelling checker, with a user definable dictionary. This may be necessary for those users who might object to certain Americanisms, like ending words in 'ize'. Of course, as the package is integrated, files can also be edited from the database and the spreadsheet.

The package has a large spreadsheet capability, up to 9999 rows and 702 columns of cells in the Plus version. It contains all the functions likely to be needed by the average user.

The additional features of Ability Plus are graphics capable of bar and line graphs and pie charts, all of which can be titled and included in word processed documents. If you add a modem to your system, it can control communications to external networks. An interesting addition to the package is 'Presentation', which allows predefined screens to be generated and used for a 'slide show', rather like the advertising displays for computers often seen in shops.

A software product evolves

A more comprehensive account of an integrated package can now be offered in relation to the PipeDream software written by Colton Software, Broadway House, 149-151 St Neot's Road, Hardwick, Cambridge, CB3 7QJ. (Telephone 0954 211472). It is remarkably efficient as an integrated piece of software. Possibly this could be due to its unique authorship by Mark Colton himself, who clearly has made a deep personal commitment to a product which has undergone a number of evolutionary developments. PipeDream's early history lay in the View word processor written for the Acorn/BBC microcomputer. As such it became a familiar and favourite tool for many people introduced to computing in that, now strangely distant era. With the improvement of the BBC micro into the Master series of machines, View itself developed into View Professional. It then rapidly evolved into PipeDream, first issued as the bundled firmware with Sir Clive Sinclair's, lapheld masterpiece, the Z88 computer. Colton Software subsequently began a process of rewriting PipeDream for various types of machine, producing an Acorn Archimedes PipeDream as well as the product which now runs on MS-DOS computers, like the Sinclair PC.

The great advantage of PipeDream is its singular ability to exchange files from one application to another. The user transfers smoothly from word processor to spreadsheet or database and back again without ever being too conscious of the move. In fact, PipeDream really does behave like one continuous program which is never abandoned, rather than distinct programs with easy file sharing.

The low price of PipeDream is also attractive. Its main disadvantage at present is the lack of graphics facilities. Colton Software are, however, working on an upgrade which will include this potential into their excellent product.

PipeDream and word processing

Word Processing with PipeDream is easy and convenient. At first the column headers might appear to be a little unusual. Rather than the dotted 'text ruler' which word processors often display at the top of the screen page, PipeDream has lettered columns, A, B, C etc., which are used in the Spreadsheet facility. This soon becomes familiar. Another minor oddity is the use of numbers to mark the left hand edge of the text displayed. A friend who accompanied the author on one occasion to the Personal Computer World Show, was a little disturbed by what she imagined were a BASIC program's line numbers appearing in the test passage with which she was practising her touch typing. Again this is an endearing little feature which is easily forgiven. Both sets of numbers are needed in PipeDream's other applications, of course. The rest of the display is truly wysiwyg.

Typing and editing of text is possible either from pull down menus called by the function keys or, once the user has become familiar with the key combinations involved, the <ALT> key plus others. Standard features, like copying and moving passages within the overall document, are all present. The format of the text can be selected and paragraphs reformed when necessary. Naturally all the conventional word processing tricks are included within PipeDream. You can switch word wrap on and off, produce a neat right hand side to your document with text justification, and search and replace particular words. Saving text is simple and also insertion of one file, which has been already saved, into another.

A further useful editing device is the way in which one passage of text can be held on the screen while another is scrolled. This will allow even easier insertion of parts of one document into another.

Underlining and boldface are available and printer drivers enable these effects to be transferred quite readily to hard copy. The manual explains carefully how to set up printer drivers to control any printer not already catered for by the package.

Colton Software have also produced a spelling checker to be employed in conjunction with PipeDream. Their SpellCheck has a vocabulary of more than 90-thousand words. It operates in two modes. It can be called from a pull-down memory and used to check the spelling of the words in a given document. Alternatively it can beep whenever it suspects the accuracy of a particular word as it is typed. Obviously this could be used as a typing tutor!

SpellCheck has a further wildcard search facility which will scan the stored dictionary for words meeting a particular set of criteria, perhaps eight letter words ending with -que. Besides crossword puzzles and various word games, this could be a fairly handy tool for junior and middle school teachers!

PipeDream spreadsheets

Spreadsheets have become such a ubiquitous aspect of personal computing that it is difficult to remember just what a novel idea they are. Their ready acceptance shows just what an essential and already existing role they were able to fulfil. Long before the arrival of microcomputers people suffered from the annoying way in which just a small alteration in a single number would affect the entire outcome of a series of calculations and require the would-be financial expert to begin all over again. Possibly the classical example of this was the mathematician who devoted his spare moments to a calculation of the irrational number pi to an impressive series of decimal places, only to discover at the end of his endeavour that a mistake had occurred at a relatively early stage...

A spreadsheet is not really appropriate for calculating pi. Two American computer programmers, Daniel Bricklin and Robert Franckston, did realise, however, that many diverse calculations involving interrelated quantities were amenable to computer intervention. Any mathematical problem which could be reduced to a table of values where individual entries were either fresh data, or quantities dependent upon other entries already in the table, could be made easier with their Visicalc program. In this, all updating of a particular entry would immediately trigger the recalculation of all other dependent values present in the table. Directly dependent positions in the table would be altered accordingly, and also those values affected in turn by the ones re-evaluated. In this way, just one alteration would provoke a wave of fresh arithmetic rippling across the entire table.

The immediate commercial success of Visicalc led to a flurry of activity as different software houses raced to develop their own similar software. A new computer application had been born. One of the most recent, and certainly one of the most effective, is PipeDream in its spreadsheet capacity.

The significance of the letters at the top of the PipeDream screen and the numbers on the left now becomes apparent when PipeDream is used as a spreadsheet. They then provide a coordinate reference to 'slots' in the document. A slot is PipeDream's equivalent to a cell in a conventional spreadsheet and functions in the same way.

When you are using PipeDream in this way, you have to specify that you are entering numerical information, or mathematical functions based upon the numerical information in other slots. This is done by making the area of the document an 'expression' slot. This can be done individually, or as a default setting for all slots. PipeDream will then realise that the information at those locations is not to be treated as bland text but, instead, as something with a specific value or a value derived mathematically from the numerical values entered into other slots.

A simple example of a spreadsheet calculation will illustrate the way in which PipeDream switches from its word processing role to that of spreadsheet. Here is a typical view of the top left corner of a document before any information has been entered:

```
. . . . . . . . . . A . . . . . . . . . . B . . . . . . . . . . C . . . . . . . . . . D . . . . . . .  .
1
2
3
4
5
```

The spreadsheet that is going to be created will calculate the total price at a photographers when a certain number of photographic prints and enlargements are ordered. First, slots A1-A5 are set up to show the relevant headings:

```
. . . . . . . . . . A . . . . . . . . . . B . . . . . . . . . . C . . . . . . . . . . D . . . . . . .  .
1  PRINT
2  ENLARGEMENT
3  No. of PR
4  No. of EN
5  TOTAL
```

Next, the price and quantity of each type of photograph is added. These are in slots B1-B4, which have to be designated expression slots in order to accept numerical values:

```
. . . . . . . . . . A . . . . . . . . . . B . . . . . . . . . . C . . . . . . . . . . D . . . . . . .
1  PRINT          0.25
2  ENLARGEMENT    6.25
3  No. of PR     24.00
4  No. of EN      3.00
5  TOTAL
```

Finally a calculation is entered into slot B5. The total is obviously the product of slots B1 and B3 added to the product of slots B2 and B4. This means that the expression B1*B3+B2*B4is typed into B5. Immediately, the total appears:

```
. . . . . . . . . . A . . . . . . . . . . B . . . . . . . . . . C . . . . . . . . . . D . . . . . . .
1  PRINT          0.25
2  ENLARGEMENT    6.25
3  No. of PR     24.00
4  No. of EN      3.00
5' TOTAL         24.75
```

The advantage of a spreadsheet can be seen. Suppose that the cost of a single print rises to 35p and you decide to reduce the number of enlargements to two to offset this increase. You simply edit the contents of slot B1 and slot B4 to obtain the new amount:

```
. . . . . . . . . . A . . . . . . . . . . B . . . . . . . . . . C . . . . . . . . . . D . . . . . . . .
1  PRINT            0.35
2  ENLARGEMENT      6.25
3  No. of PR       24.00
4  No. of EN        2.00
5  TOTAL           20.90
```

Although this is a deliberately simple example, it does reveal the potential of PipeDream.

A PipeDream database

The third application of which PipeDream is capable is a very efficient database. As with a PipeDream spreadsheet, the database facility is acquired via a standard PipeDream document and therefore permits total integration with any word processing and spreadsheet operation also being performed with the relevant material.

As an illustration of such a PipeDream database application, here is a very brief document containing information about the planets of the Solar System. The first column is the planet's name. The second gives the ratio of its mass to the Earth's. The third column is the radius of the planet in kilometres and the fourth the time it takes to orbit the Sun in days. The final column is the mean distance from the Sun in millions of kilometres:

```
. . . . . . . . . . A . . . . . . . . . . B . . . . . . . . . . C . . . . . . . . . . D . . . . . . . .
1  PLANET           MASS       RADIUS      PERIOD     DISTANCE
2  MERCURY          0.06      2425.00       88.00        58.00
3  VENUS            0.82      6070.00      225.00       108.00
4  EARTH            1.00      6378.00      365.00       150.00
5  MARS             0.11      3395.00      687.00       228.00
6  JUPITER        318.00     71600.00     4333.00       778.00
7  SATURN          95.00     60000.00    10759.00      1427.00
8  URANUS          15.00     25900.00    30685.00      2870.00
9  NEPTUNE         17.00     24750.00    60189.00      4497.00
10 PLUTO            0.11      3000.00    90465.00      5900.00
```

The information here has been entered in the familiar order of increasing distance from the Sun. However a typical operation which could be carried out on the data in PipeDream would be to sort column B into descending order. This places Jupiter first, as the most massive planet:

```
. . . . . . . . . . . A . . . . . . . . . . B . . . . . . . . . . . C . . . . . . . . . . . D . . . . . . . .
```

		MASS	RADIUS	PERIOD	DISTANCE
1	PLANET				
6	JUPITER	318.00	71600.00	4333.00	778.00
7	SATURN	95.00	60000.00	10759.00	1427.00
9	NEPTUNE	17.00	24750.00	60189.00	4497.00
8	URANUS	15.00	25900.00	30685.00	2870.00
4	EARTH	1.00	6378.00	365.00	150.00
3	VENUS	0.82	6070.00	225.00	108.00
5	MARS	0.11	3395.00	687.00	228.00
10	PLUTO	0.11	3000.00	90465.00	5900.00
2	MERCURY	0.06	2425.00	88.00	58.00

Sorting can take place numerically, as here, or alphabetically. A chronological sort is another useful feature in database work.

Rapid searching is also possible in a PipeDream database file. The user can specify the string for which the search should be performed, and include a wildcard if necessary. The range of the search can also be controlled by specifying columns or marked blocks. PipeDream allows upper and lower case to be equated or made distinct, according to user instructions.

As PipeDream loses the distinction between word processing and databases, search and replace can be used on data files. Similarly replication from the spreadsheet facility can also be used in data handling.

REFERENCES

The following are all useful material for further reading.

Exploiting MS-DOS on the AmstradPC1512

P.J.Davies and N.G.Backhurst *Sigma Press* (1987) ISBN 1 85058 0707

This is an extremely informative account of MS-DOS and goes into as much detail as you could possibly want. It has a very clear structure, dividing chapters into an initial, quick reference section and a more detailed second part. It is suitable for all IBM compatibles and so ideal for the Sinclair PC.

Operating Systems A Systematic View

William S. Davis *Addison-Wesley* (1987) ISBN 0 201 11185 3

A technical book, this is at the same time a very good overall account of the way mainframe computers use operating systems. For comparison, it also describes the use of MS-DOS and UNIX on single user systems.

A Concise Introduction to MS-DOS

N. Kantaris *Bernard Babani* (1987) ISBN 0 85934 177 1

Though a slim, pamphlet-like book, this volume does cover a great deal of material in a genuinely concise and yet understandable way.

Using DOS Plus on the AmstradPC

Stephen Morris *Glentop* (1986) ISBN 1 85181 063 3

This book will need to be read selectively so that the inappropriate parts do not confuse. Nevertheless it is an excellent description of many features of MS-DOS as well, written in a light, easily assimilated fashion.

Using GEM Paint on the AmstradPC

Stephen Morris *Heinemann New Tech* (1986) ISBN 0 434 91267 0

Again, there are some differences between the way GEM Paint is implemented on the Amstrad 1512/1640 and the Sinclair PC, but these are minimal and the exceptionally detailed explanation of various techniques given here will be extremely useful.

INDEX